The Toughest Kid We Knew

ALSO BY FRANK BERGON

Two-Buck Chuck & The Marlboro Man: The New Old West
Jesse's Ghost
Wild Game
The Temptations of St. Ed & Brother S
The Journals of Lewis and Clark, editor
Shoshone Mike
A Sharp Lookout: Selected Nature Essays of John Burroughs, editor
The Wilderness Reader, editor
The Western Writings of Stephen Crane, editor
*Looking Far West: The Search for the American West in History, Myth,
and Literature*, coeditor with Zeese Papanikolas
Stephen Crane's Artistry

The Toughest Kid We Knew

THE OLD NEW WEST

A Personal History

FRANK BERGON

UNIVERSITY OF NEVADA PRESS *Reno & Las Vegas*

University of Nevada Press | Reno, Nevada 89557 USA
www.unpress.nevada.edu
Cover photo by Lina Bergon. Author portrait by Madeline Bergon.

Library Of Congress Cataloging-In-Publication Data

Names: Bergon, Frank, author.

Title: The toughest kid we knew : the old New West :
a personal history / Frank Bergon.

Description: Reno : University of Nevada Press, [2020] | Summary: "In a companion
book to Two-Buck Chuck & The Marlboro Man, Frank Bergon presents a vivid
personal history of the place where he grew up and the people of immigrant and
migrant heritage he knew in the overlooked and most productive agricultural
region of the United States—California's San Joaquin Valley—the New West of the
twentieth century. If you want to understand how those from rural America think
and feel today, you have to read this book"—Provided by publisher.

Identifiers: LCCN 2019054905 (print) | LCCN 2019054906 (ebook) |
ISBN 9781948908641 (cloth) | ISBN 9781948908658 (ebook)

Subjects: LCSH: Cultural pluralism—California—San Joaquin Valley. | San Joaquin
Valley (Calif.)—Social life and customs—20th century. | San Joaquin Valley
(Calif.)—Social conditions—20th century.

Classification: LCC F868.S173 B47 2020 (print) |
LCC F868.S173 (ebook) | DDC 979.4/8053—dc23

LC record available at https://lccn.loc.gov/2019054905

LC ebook record available at https://lccn.loc.gov/2019054906

Grateful acknowledgment is made to the following editors for publishing portions
or shorter versions of the following essays: to Bernardo Atxaga for "My Basque
Grandmother" as "Nire amama euskalduna" in *Erlea*, to Darra Goldstein for
"Basque Family Style" as "Family Style" in *Gastronomica: The Journal of Food
and Culture*, and to Susan Shillinglaw for "Reading Steinbeck" in
John Steinbeck: Centennial Reflections by American Writers.

FIRST PRINTING
Manufactured in the United States of America

FOR MY GRANDPARENTS
Prosper Bergon and Anna Costahaude
Esteban Mendive Aurtenechea and Petra Amoroto Egaña

AND FOR MY GREAT-GRANDPARENTS
François Bergon and Marie Jeanne Noussitou
Jean Costahaude and Françoise Bergez-Benebig
Juan José Mendive Bollar and María Carmen Aurtenechea Gorguena
Evaristo Amoroto Iruretagoiena and Manuela Egaña Eizaguirre

Contents

Introduction   1

Part I: On the Ranch

My Basque Grandmother   10
Old Man Prosper   20
Reading Steinbeck   36
Seeing the Mountains   48
The Basque Nurse   57
The FBI Rancher   73
Magic in Cowboy Country   88
My L.A. Relatives   101

Part II: In the Valley

The Displaced Béarnais   114
King of the San Joaquin   122
Rose in a Country of Men   130
Chief Kit Fox Revisited   146
Reading Didion   154
Black Farm Kid and the Okies   165
The Toughest Kid We Knew   173
Basque Family Style   193

Acknowledgments   205
About the Author   207

Introduction

One June night after a late dinner in Oakland, an old friend announced to a group of us, "Your earliest memory will tell you the essential truth of your life."

We were incredulous. The essential truth of our lives? What did he mean?

He went on: "Your first memory—or the earliest one you can recall—will reveal who you really are, or at least how you see yourself and experience the world. Let's try it."

We did. The narration of our earliest memories around the table expanded beyond a parlor game as we discovered past scenes or anecdotes that became to our astonishment more enlightening than expected. We were all friends. We'd known each other for years, meaning, of course, that we had a sharper sense of each other than of ourselves. No one hesitated in choosing an early memory—whether it was literal in every detail didn't matter. Each memory had the persuasive power of a story believed by the teller. As with all stories of emotional honesty, facts gave way to truths that surprised each of us when further illuminated by the commentary of others around the table.

People's memories that night conjured up varied early experiences: the sense of luck from finding a penny, the thrill of danger at seeing a black widow spider, the sensation of mystery flickering in the shadows above a child's crib, the feeling of safety while walking with parents under shady sycamores.

I found myself talking for the first time in public about a night when I was a boy in Los Angeles, a child fresh from Nevada, on a dark, sloping lawn of a relative's house. It was my earliest memory of California. I was alone, involved in some solitary fantastical adventure, when I heard the voices of two older boys at the edge of the lawn near the sidewalk. I barely discerned their figures in the dim light. "Hey, look at this," one of the boys said. He'd picked up from the grass a wooden sword that my Basque uncle had carved for me in Nevada. It had a handle, hilt, and a curved blade painted yellow—a pirate's sword. I loved that sword. It was my favorite toy, all the more so because my favorite uncle had made it for me. "Neat," the other boy said.

I felt panic. "That's mine," I yelled.

Then the boys ran. I ran after them, but being bigger and faster they soon disappeared into the night with the sword.

The aftermath fades into dimness. I have a vague sense of myself inside the house telling my parents and relatives what had happened. I must've been crying, I must've been consoled, although I can't remember. What I recall is a hazy adult response of general sympathy enlarged by an accepting view about how such things happen in life. What more firmly remains in my mind is the dark expanse of lawn sloping downward—an odd detail for L.A.—into a deeper darkness where the thing I once cherished had now vanished.

At the Oakland dinner party, the expected Freudian interpretation of my story, initiated by one friend, was dismissed by the only professional therapist in the group, who was trained as a Jungian. The larger sense of loss described in this little story varied from person to person around the table. We all hate to lose or break things. We all have a sense of absence for the vanished lives we once lived, and every memory is tinged with its own death, an experience shared to varying degrees by those around the table that night.

When I think of my story about the sword, I recall from my childhood scrapbook a photograph of me in a pirate's costume for a Halloween party in the high desert town of Battle Mountain, Nevada. My mother took the photo. I don't remember the moment, but there I am next to my bare-bellied cousin in her veil and gauzy harem pants. A pirate's bandana covers my head. I'm wearing a blousy shirt and billowy pants. Sticking through the wide sash around my waist is the pirate's sword my uncle had carved for me. I haven't looked at the photo for years, but I remember it, and I wonder if without my memory of the photo I would've remembered that precious sword and its later loss in the way I have. Our memories, psychologists tell us, are reprints of earlier memories, like photos of photos, one layered on top of the other. What we end up remembering are memories of memories in constant flux.

For years I resisted dredging up early memories of my youth for fear of resurrecting painful experiences or hardening them into false stories. I make this admission of evasion with some regret. Because I didn't want my memories rigidified or shaped too quickly by negative feelings, I may have abandoned much of the past. Now that I've written the story of that night in California when the sword was stolen, I realize I was recounting the story as I'd narrated it to my friends in Oakland—with a few added recollections. What I'll now continue to remember, I know, is not the night as it happened—that's lost—but as it's dramatized in the words of the story I've written.

Sometimes in my dreams I hear the voices of my mother or father with such intensity that I'm startled upon awakening to discover that my parents are dead. Such dreams in their sound and motion can generate an emotional truthfulness beyond the factual accuracy of photographs. In the profiles and essays that follow, I've tried to offer glimpses of a way of life on ranches and small towns of the mid-twentieth century, put into motion and sound through their telling with something of a dream's truth. As the past bubbled to mind with certain long-ago events

I hadn't thought of in years, I sensed something akin to the claim of the eighteenth-century writer Thomas De Quincey: "Of this, at least, I feel assured, that there is no such thing as *forgetting* possible to the mind."

To preserve against loss or to recover lost events, lost histories, and lost stories is what writers do, whether one is Willa Cather in New York City remembering the Great Plains of her childhood in *A Lost Lady* or a Frenchman in a fifth-floor Paris apartment fashioning seven volumes *In Search of Lost Time*. To write as a way of discovery and preservation can give glimpses into the felt texture of other lives, as I realized that night in Oakland when facts shared with those around a table grew into unexpected truths.

My concern in this book is primarily with California's San Joaquin Valley, in the center of the state, where I grew up on my Béarnais American grandfather's Madera County ranch. I wrote about this valley in an earlier book, *Two-Buck Chuck & The Marlboro Man: The New Old West*, as a place where frontier values shared by a multiracial and multiethnic population gave the valley its distinctive character and in many ways continue to do so beyond the physical transformations of technology and modernity in the twenty-first century. In this companion book, I move back in time to write about my own family and boyhood community, people whose stories also include a variety of immigrants and migrants, as well as their offspring, many shaped as I was in small towns and on family ranches. What follows isn't an autobiography or a traditional memoir. It's a book about community and communal memory, an attempt through personal essays and profiles of people I've known, including my own family, to help understand how it felt and what it meant to be alive in a particular place at a particular time. I soon discovered that I was writing about something else: Western life ignored or misrepresented in most histories of California and the West. In a time calling for an understanding of rural America, what emerges for me in these stories is a way of life that continues to be dismissed or remain invisible in the larger culture. These are stories of rural and small-town Westerners, who helped shape California, the New West, and America itself, people whose stories point to how those from rural America think and feel today.

The California of my boyhood led the way in making the "New West" a place of suburban tract ranch homes, shopping centers, supermarkets, drive-in theaters, and trend-setting clothes, including Levi's with copper rivets originally invented for working men by a Latvian Jewish immigrant and a California company a hundred years earlier. "Don't Californicate Our State," other Westerners hollered. But it was useless. California, as the extreme West, showed the way the urban-and-suburban West was going and simply got there first. The Santa Clara Valley, where I went to high school, was a region of flowering fruit trees nicknamed Valley of Heart's Delight before it dissolved into Silicon Valley, where overpriced real estate, computer chips, and start-ups replaced apricots and cherries in the latest rush for gold. The rural San Joaquin Valley remained a place where the lingering Old West intersected with the New West. Now viewed from the twenty-first century, the valley of my boyhood appears in sepia hues as the Old New West.

Other people's voices and memories appear in this portrayal of the West, as noted in the "We" of the book's title. In their stories, both old-timers and newcomers in this book relate overlapping experiences and shared beliefs. My immigrant Basque grandmother in Nevada shares something with the migrant Okie we knew as the toughest kid in the valley. *Indarra* is the word in Euskara applied to my grandmother and other Basques for their persistence, endurance, and strength. Toughness as a primary virtue is what Okie boys and girls understood not simply as physical strength for fighting and work but an ability to endure. My California-born grandfather, who was a tenant farmer in the early twentieth century, could talk with a migrant African American landowner and an immigrant fieldworker fifty years later because they shared a belief in the rewards of perseverance, an allegiance to Western dreams of freedom and opportunity, and an expectation of diversity and porous social-class boundaries, all co-existing with an abiding acceptance of disappointment.

My old writing teacher at Stanford, Wallace Stegner, once said, "I suspect that a sharecropper and a banker in Charlotte, North Carolina, have more in common than a banker in North Carolina and a banker in Redwood City." Stegner was talking about a shared regional culture as an important force in our lives. It certainly was when my father and aunt went to a valley school whose pupils represented a mixed heritage of Japanese, Italian, German, Mexican, Chinese, Basque, Béarnais, African, Assyrian, Swedish, Portuguese, Russian, and Armenian, born inside or outside the state, though all Californians, whose view of themselves didn't stop at the border. Connections remained even for me with relatives in Nevada, the Basque Country, and Béarn. Others of my generation give accounts of the porous social borders we lived in, as when the son of a Jewish doctor made his first visit to a classmate's home that turned out to be at a labor tent camp. The valley remains one of the most racially and ethnically rich areas in the country, but Stegner's claim of a shared culture and mine of shared experiences have less verity in the current valley of gated communities and suburban isolation.

As a descendant of immigrants, I'm aware of how the valley's diverse population can challenge conventional views of California and the West. As a ranch boy, I'm aware of how the valley's many family farms can upend the stereotype of corporate factories in the field. The rural values that emerge in this book sometimes created a shared cultural environment, as Stegner suggested, but a region is composed of both cultural and physical environments that intertwine. We don't know much about the formative power of our physical environment. At least I don't. We know more about how we shape it than about how it shapes us. Sometimes presented as trivial examples of the power of place are the regional flavors of bagels, sourdough bread, wine, and cigars, which may not be so trivial after all. In the smells and sounds of the ranch air where I lived as a boy I felt the physical power of the land as an active agent in my life. Atmospheric changes weren't just shifts in weather but expressions of the land's spirit, something I felt but didn't realize until I moved away and the natural world began to function as a character in my novels—maybe the chief character—and their source of value.

Today a way of thinking remains in the valley, renewed as in the past by immigrants and migrants, but a particular rural experience is gone. Rapid change is a common trait writers ascribe to the San Joaquin Valley and to California itself. There the American way of extirpating the past and violently altering the land is accelerated. California remains home to some people, like my sisters, while to others it's a place to live without ever feeling at home. Or it's a former home, as for my brother and me. Nostalgia doesn't drive my return to that world. Some things in the past were better, some weren't. In the paternalistic ranch world where I grew up, a culture of fighting, ignorance about alcoholic addiction, brutalizing labor, and a feudal mentality created much pain better lost and bid good riddance. Memories also remain of rural beauty, small-town camaraderie, fair play, love of the land, enjoyment of its food, and joy in hard work done well. What I write is a personal history of a past and people shaping the country I called home.

I

On the Ranch

My Basque Grandmother

From the beginning I called her "Grandma." I had only one grandma because my California grandmother, who emigrated from France's Barétous Valley, died before I was born. Grandma lived far away over the mountains in the high desert of Nevada, strangely distant from who we were in the San Joaquin Valley. I'd been born in Nevada, a wild landscape I loved and connected to the Old West, while in California I sensed myself part of a burgeoning New West. My California family ranched in a verdant irrigated valley, while my Nevada cousins ran cattle in dry sagebrush country. In Battle Mountain, Grandma embodied the disconnection I felt between these two worlds. She rolled her r's with a heavy foreign accent. She wore old-fashioned, shapeless dresses that buttoned down the front. She'd been born in far-off Spain. Hardship and suffering though she'd endured all her life, her warm, cheerful face emerged amid tight curls of gray hair, big eyeglasses, and a constant smile because she loved everyone. She was my Basque grandmother, *mi abuela vieja, nire amama euskalduna*.

In the San Joaquin Valley, we were Americans first, Westerners second. My parents had never traveled to Europe and didn't want to. When pressed for my heritage, I usually said with the accepted euphemism of the time, "Half-French, half-Spanish," or I would reply "Mostly French" to questions about my family name because that was the easier side of the family to explain. French was the nationality of my father, aunt, and grandfather on the ranch, although I didn't know then that they, too, were part Basque. To be a mixture of backgrounds was so typically American that I felt no oddness in asking my mother's brother how much the Spanish side of our family was Basque. "All of it," he snapped.

But what was a Basque? One afternoon, the Basque American writer Robert Laxalt and I sprawled outside on the grass next to his Nevada home, as he was accustomed to do after lunch, in the manner of sheepherders. "When I was growing up," Laxalt told me, "I didn't know what the hell a Basque was." Although he spoke Basque as a child, he said he knew nothing about Basque history or culture until his late twenties when he took his father back to the Basque Country. Laxalt put into words my own knowledge as a child. I ate at the Basque Hotel, I saw Basque herders with their flocks in our winter fields, and I had a Basque mother and grandmother, but I didn't know what the hell a Basque was.

In the beginning I knew Grandma as the matriarch of my Basque family in America. Her name was Petra Amoroto Egaña, and she married Esteban Mendive Aurtenechea, a grandfather I knew only through photos and stories. He'd died the year after I was born. Like Laxalt, when I traveled to the Basque Country I learned about culture and history, but more, I met my relatives there and learned about my grandparents as Basques in their homeland. With my wife, Holly, and a cousin, Bernardo Arrizabalaga Amoroto, a novelist in the Basque Country, I discovered in the sacristy of the hilltop church in Ajangiz, overlooking Gernika, an old ledger on a dusty shelf containing the handwritten record of my grandfather's birth and baptism on the day after Christmas in 1873. After Bernardo laboriously copied the document with his pen, which he would later type up for us, he tracked down the parish priest in the rectory, and with the vehement authority he mustered as a former Jesuit, he reprimanded and urged the ultimately obliging priest to move the valuable baptismal records from the open shelf to someplace safe.

No one in the village of Ajangiz remembered my grandfather, except an ancient blind woman named Claudia, sitting with a cane in silence by a fire, refusing the company of even a radio, she explained, because she had her memories. "I've heard something of him," she told us about my grandfather, who was an only son and whose sisters entered the Ursuline convent, "but he went away to America." In 1897, when he was twenty-three, he sailed to the United States out of Cherbourg, France, on the SS *Normannia*.

In America, Esteban followed the immigrant's dream up the ladder of success. In those years, after the Comstock Lode silver mining boom, Nevada had a higher proportion of foreign-born residents than any other state in the country, higher even than second-place California or New York, with immigrants coming from nearly forty countries and five continents. Esteban worked first as a sheepherder, as did most Basques, even when they might have been fishermen in the Basque Country and known nothing about sheep. Some migrated from California as out-of-luck miners, but most, like Esteban, came directly from the Basque Country. He herded sheep in Paradise Valley, north of Winnemucca, before going to work at the mines as a muleskinner—western lingo for muleteer—driving ore wagons and saving his wages to become a merchant and hotel owner in the ranching and copper-mining town of Battle Mountain. According to family legend, when he was thirty-four, he met a Basque sheepherder from Markina, who had some photographs from his hometown. One photo caught Esteban's attention.

"Who's that girl?" he asked.

"Her name's Petra Amoroto."

"She looks pretty cute."

"She's even more so than she looks here."

This imagined conversation was published in my cousin Bernardo's newspaper column in the Basque Country after our travels around Bizkaia in search of our shared past. Bernardo continued to narrate the remarkable conclusion to this story. One day in Markina, young Petra received a letter from America. Because her mother had died and her father, a schoolteacher and municipal secretary, was struggling with depression, Petra lived with her aunt and uncle, Bernardo's future grandparents. Along with her cousin Raimunda—Bernardo's future mother—Petra worked as a maid and serving girl for a rich family in town. With the letter in her hand, she approached her uncle. She spoke to him in Euskara.

—*Begira zazu zer diñoustan mutil batek Ameriketatik.* "Look at what a boy is asking me from America."

—*Zer diñoutsu ba?* "What's he telling you?"

The young girl handed the letter to her uncle, who read a marriage proposal from Esteban Santos Mendive.

—*Zugaz eskondu nahi dau.* "He wants to marry you."

—*Bai.* "Yes."

—*Eta zuk, zer diñozu?* "And what do you think?"

—*Horrexegaitik nator zuregana.* "That's why I'm coming to you."

Her uncle told her that she wasn't going to America to get married. She would first get married at home by proxy and then go to America. Esteban's father stood in for his son during the ceremony. First she would marry the father, then the son. When Petra's cousin learned that the girl who was like her sister was leaving for America, she angrily took Petra's framed photo on her bureau and turned it to face the wall.

Petra was twenty-one when she made her way to Liverpool and took the SS *Teutonic* to New York to meet a thirty-five-year-old, blue-eyed Basque stranger from the West as a mail-order bride. I can only imagine the excitement and fear jumping in her stomach as she left the Basque Country and traveled alone first to England and then sailed across the ocean. At Ellis Island she was described as five-seven, in good health, with dark brown hair, brown eyes, and ten dollars. According to a family story, she'd written Esteban to describe what she would be wearing when she arrived in New York, but he didn't show up, as he'd said he would. Instead, there was a message for her to meet him out west in Utah. According to the story, she sent Esteban a telegram saying that if he wasn't in Utah to meet her she was going to turn around and go home.

On the long train ride across the country, knowing no English, she could communicate her requests in the dining car with only two four-syllable Spanish words, *en-sa-la-da* and *cho-co-la-te*. As a sign of identification when she stepped off the train at the Ogden station, she wore a brooch on her breast, ready to get married again. According to *La historia de los Vascongados en el Oeste de los Estados Unidos* (1917), *la señorita Petra Amoroto y el señor Mendive* were officially united in the holy bonds of matrimony in Ogden, Utah. The date was January 17, 1909.

That girl of incredible steel, who crossed the Atlantic and the United States by herself, seems strangely disconnected from the plump, cheerful grandmother in owlish glasses I knew as a boy in Battle Mountain, where unpaved streets were speckled with turquoise mixed in the gravel. I remember as a child the distinctive, rich smells from her wood-fired kitchen stove drifting through her two-story house, the soups I ate in a heavy white bowl on a table covered with an oilcloth. In the morning, she filled my bowl with chunks of homemade bread, soaked in hot coffee, milk, and lots of sugar, called *sopesniak*, but this was after we'd gone outside to feed the "pidgies" in her big pigeon coop. No one snapped a chicken's neck quicker before plucking. The warm attention I thought Grandma directed only to me, I came to learn, was a childhood delusion shared with my sisters, brother, and numerous cousins, in short, all her grandchildren. The ease I felt with Grandma as a child, knowing she'd welcome

me with a smile anytime I showed up, extended through ado-
lescence into young adulthood. When I stopped overnight in
Battle Mountain with three friends during a cross-country drive
after graduating from college, my grandmother was up the next
morning frying chicken on the wood stove, loads of it, for us to
take in the car. "This is the best fried chicken I've ever eaten,"
a classmate kept repeating, and the others agreed, as we drove
to California, an acclamation that startled me at the time—I'd
assumed that was the way all grandmothers cooked.

I remember sitting with her as a child in the living room of our
California ranch house, where beyond the bay window and the
eucalyptus trees in our front yard stretched a spring pasture and
a herd of white-faced Hereford cattle, while she patiently showed
me the intricacies of crocheting—I wanted to learn—and felt no
shame as a boy in giving it a try. What I remember beyond her
smile and patience was the simple pleasure of sitting next to her.
She spoke to me in Spanish and taught me a few words in Euskara.

What I didn't know at the time was that Euskara, or Basque,
was the oldest language in Europe, with no connection to any
other living language in the world. I later learned that a speaker of
Euskara was called an *Euskaldun*. Speakers of the language were
also called *Vascos* in Spanish, and *Basques* in English and French,
because the words were derived from Latin *Vascones* or *Vasconum*,
but I didn't know why the Romans came up with these names
for the tribal ancestors in my grandmother's home country. Only
years later when I dusted off my high school and college Latin and
Greek did I discover that the early Roman historians were phonet-
ically reproducing what the people called themselves.

I saw in the first-century *Geography* by the Greco-Roman historian Strabo the earliest surviving names of these pre-Roman
people recorded as Οὐάσκνων and Οὐάσκνας. The Roman historian Livy called them *Vasconum*. In the next century Ptolemy

wrote *Ouascones*. Others wrote *Vascones*. Now words that look so different have similar sounds if we remember that V in Latin was probably pronounced like a soft W or U. As I was taught in school, Caesar's famous "*Veni, Vidi, Vici*" ("I came, I saw, I conquered") was pronounced closer to "Ueni, Uidi, Uiki." The Latin for *Vasconum* would then be pronounced closer to "Uasconum" or the Greek *Ouaskonon*. Both the Latin and the Greek are close phonetic spellings of what a contemporary Basque woman might call herself in the Markina dialect of my grandmother: "Ouskunan," or "Euskunan," meaning someone who has or speaks Euskara. What makes this research fascinating to me was that two thousand years ago this pre-Roman people defined themselves with the same words as do many contemporary Basques. Recent archaeologists have also discovered that some modern Basques, perhaps like my grandmother, were found to share DNA links with ancient Basque farmers buried three thousand years before the Roman Empire.

Looking back, I now wonder what my grandmother felt when looking at our pastoral ranch landscape of green corn and cotton with flowing irrigation ditches, Hereford and Angus cattle grazing in pastures, so unlike the harsh sagebrush desert she encountered as an immigrant girl. What happened when she arrived in the Nevada desert, also so different from the shiny green hills of her home in the Basque Country? Did she cry, as did many Basque sheepherders when facing the loneliness of the high desert in contrast to the green memories of their homeland? Or was she simply too busy, working and having babies? She had eight of them: Maria Carmen, Lina Rose, Julia Petra, Pedro Rufino, Elissa Antonia, Angela Victoria, Neva Teresa, and Luis Esteban Justino.

She was living in Battle Mountain in 1911, the year my mother was born, when out in the nearby desert a posse of buckaroos on horseback tracked down and massacred Shoshone Mike and his family. Burned into my consciousness as a boy was how this so-called last Indian massacre of the West's pioneering era was so recent, with the vanished Old West bleeding into the New West not far from my grandmother's house in a time of telephones, electricity, automobiles, and even airplanes. Haunted by this story, I would later go on to spend ten years in researching and writing a historical novel about it.

None of Petra's children married other Basques, though some of their offspring did, the bloodlines of their intermarriages typical of a West in the making. My mother, Lina Rose, married the son of a Béarnais American rancher in the San Joaquin Valley, while her sister, Julia, married a rancher, Joe Filippini, whose Swiss Italian father was described in an Elko editorial as a pioneer Nevada stockman. Immigrant Italians, Germans, and Basques largely settled northern Nevada, with many Italians emigrating from the old Tuscan duchy of Lucca and from Switzerland to become cowboys and ranchers. Uncle Joe was a cowboy, rancher, and also my godfather. An old photo from Uncle Joe's ranch shows my cousin Joanna and me as kids, dressed in winter coats and stocking caps, together carrying a milk bucket from the barn across the snow. Another shows us on an empty hay wagon, with me sadly looking downward with folded hands. A splinter in one hand was hurting, but I hadn't told anyone. I knew the code, dramatically emphasized years later when Uncle Lou told his four-year-old grandson after he tripped, fell, and bloodied his nose, "Big boys don't cry."

West of the ranch in Battle Mountain was the grocery store Esteban had bought on Front Street and expanded into E.S. Mendive's Cash Store and General Merchandise, adding a second floor to the brick building to serve as the Mendive Hotel, later renamed the Midway Hotel for its location on the railroad stop halfway between Ogden and Sacramento. Behind the store before Petra's arrival, he'd built for her the town's first two-story brick home. The store advertised first-class groceries, hardware, flour, and grain, as well as ladies' and gents' furnishings, and supplies for miners and ranchers. The store catered to Basques in the desert with stacks of *bacalao*, the salted cod they'd loved in their homeland, and strong, dark coffee. I now have in my kitchen the store's big hand-crank coffee grinder. Customers drank more than coffee, especially in summer. In June 1910, Esteban wired an order for the Becker Brewing & Malting Company in Ogden to ship him "at once" 120 barrels of beer. That's a lot of beer—3,720 gallons.

After Esteban's death in 1944, his son Pedro Rufino, now called Pete, ran the store, but my grandmother ran the hotel and continued running it until her own death in 1975. For years she hauled soiled sheets down the narrow, steep hotel stairs and back to the house, where she washed them in an old squeeze-roll wringer-washer before hanging them on the clothesline. When Holly and I were helping to paint the hotel rooms one summer, my uncle told us how he was repairing the hotel's roof and my grandmother, who was eighty-seven, crawled through a window and onto the roof to help him. I realized then that the young girl of steel and my grandmother were the same person.

"I think Grandma had a lot on her plate," my brother told me, "though she didn't show it." Madness, breakdowns, drunkenness, and early death struck several of her adult children. Her grandson James—my cousin—was a Marine killed in the Quàng Nam Province of Vietnam. He was nineteen. His name is on the wall. A granddaughter—my cousin Joanna from our childhood ranch days—and her husband, with five young children at home at the time, died when their small plane, loaded with ore from their turquoise mine, crashed in the mountains. The town park in Battle Mountain is named in honor of these cousins. Another grandson—my cousin George—was robbed and murdered in

Las Vegas. My grandmother went to Mass every morning. She wrote to relatives in the Basque Country after my mother died unexpectedly: "The more you think about some things the less you know." An alcoholic daughter, after several husbands, divorces, and lovers—a sweet aunt to me—lived with my grandmother when my younger sister was visiting in Battle Mountain. Grandma was watering her garden when our aunt emerged from the house all decked out and carrying a little suitcase. Grandma asked her where she was going. "I don't remember the reply," my sister told me, "but Grandma said, 'You're not going anywhere.'" And then our sweet, steely grandmother turned the hose on her daughter. "Now *that*," my sister said, "is embedded in my memory."

My relatives in the Basque Country remember when my grandmother was in her sixties and returned to Bizkaia for a year's visit. They have several letters from her in America. In one, though the translation loses the pun, she wrote, this isn't *los Estados Unidos* (the United States), it's *los Estados Jodidos* (the Fucked-up States).

Some years after her death, five of us American grandchildren visited our relatives in the Basque Country. A cousin in Markina distributed pieces of family silverware my grandmother ate with as a child. Every night at my dinner table I see a serving spoon and fork engraved with the initials *AE* for the joined family names of her parents, Evaristo Amoroto Iruretagoiena and Manuela Egaña Eizaguirre. I imagine some of her other grandchildren in the West seeing the same initials, as do some of her relatives sharing her name in the Basque Country, pointing to the moral of this story about my Basque family: it's our Basque grandmother who connects us—to our past, yes, but also to each other in the present.

Old Man Prosper

We all lived together in a ranch house—my father, mother, sisters, brother, grandfather, aunt, and me—but the name stenciled on ranch lug boxes made it clear who was in charge—"P. Bergon." Most of the ranch workers called him "Pete," my parents called him "Pop," but his real name was Prosper, and prosper he did. Out of his hearing, people respectfully called him the "Old Man." To me he was "Grandpa," the man I slept with in the same bed, the man I thought I knew better than the rancher and patriarch who was called all those other names, until he was gone and I began to piece together the sides that mysteriously made up the person called P. Bergon, Prosper, Pete, Pop, Old Man, and Grandpa.

Grandpa was stocky and square-jawed, with silver hair combed straight back, who in many ways fit the stereotypical stoic Westerner, deliberate in action and given to few words. Almost every morning Grandpa ate a bowl of Kix, silently for the most part, except for a smacking of lips. I felt comfortable with his reserve because he wasn't the boss to me as he was to others, more wary in their admiration, even among our family whose affection for him was no less than mine. "We'll wait and see" was his common response to so many proposals from my father, mother, and aunt that they joked about changing the name of the ranch. My dad said he would get a weight from the cattle scales and design a new brand for the Weight & C Ranch.

To them his name was familiarly Pop, never the Old Man. "Old" was an honorific title in the West, as I learned in my reading about mountain men like Jim Bridger, who was called "Old Gabe." As a boy I'd come to use the term in place of "Mr." for several aging men who worked for my grandfather and populated my boyhood as model ranch hands and storytellers with time to entertain a kid eager for stories and sometimes even to help him out. One sunny summer morning when I was five years old, I found myself stuck in mud and water up to my thighs, unable to move, in the middle of a vineyard a country mile from my house—I was always wandering alone through fields—when Old Man Lascurain, the Mexican irrigator with a surname of Basque ancestry, appeared among the vines like a smiling straw-hatted angel, wearing irrigation boots and carrying a shovel on his shoulder, to dig me free.

Old Dad Irwin, my grandfather's former foreman and horseman, told me stories for hours. I have a black-and-white photo of him and me, both in Levi's and straw hats, under the pecan tree in front of a ranch house, where he continued to live long after he was too old to break and shoe horses for my grandfather. Old Man Lascurain and Old Pancho Gonzales died in their houses on the ranch, while Old Dad Irwin eventually ended up in a nursing home. A small, wiry man with a white Mark Twain mustache, he told me stories while shelling pecans with fingers surprisingly big-knuckled from his years of working the forge and pounding horseshoes in the blacksmith shop across the yard. Cracked shells fell to the ground. Nuts got tossed into a big silver bucket. A black dog at his feet in the photo appears attentive to the old man's stories as well.

The storyteller who told me most about my grandfather was Old Man Blasingame, who, after years away from the ranch, returned with a son fresh out of prison and a wife with interminable hiccups. He needed work, and my dad sent me, now a teenager, out to help him irrigate cotton and alfalfa because he was so old. He didn't need my help. The legendary strength and toughness of his youth seemed little diminished. His stories broadened my sense of how others saw my grandfather. He told me about his coming to the valley as a young man from Oklahoma in the 1930s and asking who in the area was the best farmer. "They told me P. Bergon was the best farmer," he said. "I drove out to his ranch and found some workers in a hayfield." It was a blistering summer day. Old Man Blasingame asked the hayers where he could find P. Bergon. "One of the workers came up to me—sweat was pouring out his trouser legs like water from a hose—and he said to me, 'I'm P. Bergon,' and I told him, 'I come to work for you.'"

The man others called Prosper began ranching in the San Joaquin Valley as a tenant farmer—a form of sharecropping—when he was twenty-four, after moving from Los Angeles, where he'd farmed with his Béarnais father. As young as eight, Prosper drove horses on a hay baler. His father, François Bergon, was born in the mountain village of Arette in the Pyrenees, twenty miles from the Pic de Bergon, and had come to California from Béarn in 1878 after serving in the Franco-Prussian War. He lost many sheep during a dry year, sold the rest, and moved his family to Palms to raise wheat. *The History of Fresno County* (1919) reports that Prosper, who was born in Riverside, "received a good education in the schools in Palms." He was fluent in French, Béarnaise, and Spanish, and could get along in Italian, languages he learned out of school. In a partnership with his father, he leased Rancho La Brea from Old Lady Hancock, as he called her, in what is now Hollywood and Wilshire's Miracle Mile in downtown Los Angeles.

An advertising flyer of 1912 shows a photo of "A Sandwich Belt Power Hay Press in Operation. Owned by Prosper Bergon, Los Angeles, Cal." The flip side of the ad has these words:

Words of Praise for the Sandwich Presses
Los Angeles, Cal., May 10, 1912
Hawley King & Co.,
Los Angeles, Cal.

Gentlemen:

After using one of your SOUTHWICK HORSE
POWER HAY PRESSES for four years, during which
time I baled as high as forty tons in one day, and
averaged 32 tons per day, I sold the press for $225.00
and last year I bought one of your 18X22 SANDWICH
BELT PRESSES with Friction Clutch. I equipped this
press with a derrick and spool and averaged 52 tons
per day for the entire season.

This is a moneymaking outfit and I cheerfully recom-
mend it to any one who wants to bale hay for a profit.

Yours truly,

(Signed) PROSPER BERGON

The photograph on this company-generated testimonial
shows Prosper in overalls in a hayfield, indistinguishable from
the other workers holding pitchforks—one is waving a hat—atop
a stack of baled hay, except that Prosper is standing front and
center, leg cocked, smiling, with his hand resting proprietarily
on the long belt of a newfangled stationary hay baler, with no
houses in sight, only a cook wagon and horses, in a vast field
with hills in the distance of what is now urbanized Los Angeles.

"Your grandfather always owned the latest equipment,"
my cousin Henry told me, "and was always trying the newest
things." Prosper was then twenty-four and newly married to
Anna Costahaude, who was born in Béarn and immigrated to Los

Angeles when she was sixteen to work as a servant for the family of John Byrne, a Santa Fe Railroad executive. Through the local Béarnais network and her brother Jean Pierre, who'd emigrated from Feas a year earlier, she met and married Prosper when she was nineteen. A year later she was pregnant with their first child.

That same year, 1912, Prosper sold out to his father and leased from James Gallagher 850 acres in Kerman along the San Joaquin River, where he operated a dairy, grew alfalfa and grain, and raised Percheron and Belgian draft horses.

One of the leases stipulated how in exchange for his use of the land P. Bergon "shall in the best and most approved and skillful husbandlike manner" grow, irrigate, cut, and harvest alfalfa; pump water; care and provide fuel for the water pump; and deliver to Gallagher one-half of all the alfalfa he produces and one-quarter of any grain. The grain was to be delivered in sacks.

On Sundays, Prosper cut the hair of workmen and neighbors and half-soled their shoes. He had a regular shoe shop going. He went to other ranches to castrate horses, hogs, calves, sheep, and even tomcats. He tossed the cats upside down into a rubber boot to stabilize them before cutting. On Sunday afternoons he and Anna picnicked on the river with their children and neighbors. My dad remembered going with milk buckets to pick mushrooms along the San Joaquin River. He and Prosper and Anna would string and hang them behind the woodstove to dry so they had mushrooms all year. With no refrigeration, Anna stored chickens, geese, ducks, and all the birds Prosper shot in barrels of lard as a way of preserving them.

In 1920 Prosper moved his family to Madera County and became a landowner. Starting out with forty acres of raw land, he planted a vineyard and grew cotton between the young vine rows, making him one of the earliest cotton pioneers in the area. He acquired more ranches, especially during the Depression.

"The banks knew your grandfather was a good farmer," Cousin Henry told me, "and they'd buy him any ranch he wanted without a down payment." In honor of his lender he named one of his ranches the Bank Ranch. "He got the Bank Ranch cheap," Cousin Henry said, "with no money down." He bought other ranches with pastureland for cattle and sheep and eventually built one of the first automated feedlots in the San Joaquin Valley. Besides the thousand acres he eventually owned, he leased other ranches with several partners.

During the Depression, Anna raised and sold turkeys, shipping them as far away as Los Angeles and earning enough money on her own to install an indoor bathroom while Prosper still used the wooden outhouse in the backyard. In 1928, Anna's sister-in-law in L.A. ordered a Thanksgiving turkey "about 12 to 14 lb dressed," and two more "young ones" of the same weight for relatives, knowing in those years the best size for good-tasting birds. Sidney Epstein remembers riding his horse as a boy from town out to the ranch for lunch. His dad, Sam Epstein, owned Money Back Sam, a men's clothes and furnishing store on the town's main street, Yosemite Avenue. Sam and Prosper had come to Madera County the same year and were good friends. On Sunday Sam drove his horse and buggy out to the ranch, while Sidney rode ahead on horseback. Anna would put cream and fresh fruit in a hand-crank ice cream freezer, packed with ice and rock salt—she was renowned for her peach ice cream. "I would easily and happily turn the handle," Sidney wrote in reminiscence. "No ice cream has ever been as good. A memory so strong, I still think I can taste its cool, creamy fruit flavors and wonderful richness. What a memory and experience!"

Floating his ranches in a universe of loans, Prosper, like all ranchers, could find himself in money trouble after a single year of bad weather, destroyed crops, and poor prices. If all your money is tied up in crops and you don't get it back, you're in money trouble. In 1924, an epidemic of equine encephalitis hit the valley and killed the horses. All of my grandfather's best horses were wiped out. It was the only time my dad saw my grandfather cry. In 1929, the disease hit again. Cash was short during the Depression, and the story goes that Prosper told his workers he could keep them in food and clothes and would pay them later. His fellow Béarnais American Jean Sagouspe told me he herded sheep for my grandfather without pay. Afterward, my grandfather put him through barber college in Oakland. Ranch hands ate at a big table with the family, including the turbaned Sikh irrigators, many formerly in the British army. Without pay, the workers built a large modern machine shop with a concrete floor and an automobile repair pit. Loaded with debt, my grandfather saved what was called the Big Ranch by putting it in the name of his friend Sam Epstein until better times enabled him to take it back.

In 1932, Anna had a tooth infection that spread to her brain, causing an abscess. She was taken to San Francisco for an operation, but the brain abscess burst and she died. She was thirty-nine.

Three years later, in Reno, Nevada, Prosper married the divorced wife of a neighboring farmer, whose name was Jessie. The new Mrs. Bergon moved to the ranch with a son in high school. My dad played the violin with Jessie, who played the piano. She taught my dad's sister—my aunt Evelyn—to play the piano and gave lessons to country kids, including the Mochizuki children, before they were sent off to a Japanese internment camp.

In other ways Jessie remains a shadowy figure in our family lore, rarely mentioned, except in unhappy ways. My father, who'd left home soon after Jessie moved in, implied his stepmother had become emotionally unstable. Cousin Henry indirectly buttressed his judgment of Jessie by attributing it to his beloved mother, who was Prosper's aunt. "My mother sure didn't like Jessie," Cousin Henry told me. "Your grandfather paid for her boy to go to UCLA." This negative view came from relatives who'd all loved Anna, Prosper's French-and-Béarnais speaking immigrant wife.

Jessie's son told me that Prosper's affair with his mother had begun before her divorce, so who knows if he was faithful to her? Her son quickly added that Proper was always good to him and he'd heard nothing specific about another woman, and none appeared. Maybe the difference between Anna and Jessie was too much of a jump. Whatever happened, the marriage soured.

After the Second World War, and eleven years of marriage, Prosper returned home from a fall deer hunting trip to discover Jessie had taken his new Dodge and left the ranch. A newspaper article in 1947 announced: "Wealthy Maderan Is Sued For Divorce—Mrs. Jessie Lois Bergon today filed suit for divorce from Prosper J. Bergon, wealthy Madera County farmer." Jessie asked for a monthly allowance of $750 until settlement of the ranches she said they owned in common, worth nearly a million dollars. The court granted her $250 a month. He kept the ranches.

During the turmoil with Jessie, my parents moved us from Nevada back to the valley to live with my grandfather, partly for my father to help with the ranches and the machinations of the divorce. I was too young to learn anything about my step-grandmother, and I never met her, but I did meet men who lived on the ranch and worked for my grandfather for decades. A cowboy named Bob Smith had taken over for Old Dad Irwin as ranch foreman until he himself would eventually become Old Bob Smith. Old Pancho Gonzales and Old Man Lascurain still irrigated. The loyalty of these men to my grandfather was certainly connected to the plantation economics and feudal mentality of ranch life at the time, but it also arose from the way their lives intertwined with a rancher they admired. Some had lost their own land back in Oklahoma and Arkansas during the Depression, or in Mexico during the revolution, causing them to identify with the struggles of a fellow farmer. Old Bunk Childers would talk to my dad about the alfalfa he irrigated as "my field" and "my water."

Old Man Blasingame took a protective stance toward the land when he confronted some poachers on the ranch. "This is Mr. P. Bergon's property," he told the three men, who held shotguns. "You have to get off."

They told him to go fuck himself.

Too old to fight them, Old Man Blasingame told the men with guns, "Just stand right there. Don't move." He reached through the open window of their car, removed the keys from the ignition, and walked away to call the sheriff.

Not all the men admired my grandfather the way Old Man Blasingame did. When the big four-bay machine shop built during the Depression burned down, a disgruntled worker was suspected. Old Man Blasingame said he'd once seen my grandfather go out into a field to fire a drunken irrigator. On the ditch bank, the angry irrigator swung his shovel blade at my grandfather's head, but my grandfather grabbed the shovel with one hand and slugged the man in the jaw with his fist, knocking him to the ground.

"He was tough," Cousin Henry told me. "He would tackle anything."

This tough, fiery rancher was not the grandpa I knew. As my main Western model and mentor, he was the man who knew how to do things and expected the same of others. I loved riding in the car with him, even though he drove more slowly down country roads than anyone I knew. The way he shifted gears from low into third, skipping second, reinforced my sense of his know-how and uniqueness (no one else I knew did that). He avoided both waste and wasted motion. I used to watch him dip a pen into a bottle of ink and write checks at his enormous golden-oak rolltop desk. If the nib made a blot on the check or if he made a mistake, he took out his penknife, licked the small blade, and carefully scraped the paper surface of the check to remove the error before writing over it. I now write checks on the same rolltop desk but simply void the ones I botch.

"I learned a lot from Old Pete," my dad's foreman, Sonny Clement, later told me, "just riding around in the car with him. A lot of people think your dad hired me, but it was really Pete." Sonny was twenty-three years old and working for another rancher when he happened to meet my grandfather with some workmen raking hay at the Bank Ranch. "He was trying to figure out how to get the hay dry enough to hog it for the feedlot," Sonny said. Loose hay needed to be real dry or the big stack by the feed mill was in danger of catching fire from spontaneous combustion, as had happened. Sonny suggested using rigs with wheels to raise the windrows from the damp ground without turning the hay over so it could dry for a couple of hours before the big hogger came in.

"Who do you work for?" my grandfather asked Sonny.

Sonny told him.

"Not anymore," my grandfather said.

On the ranch, after a roundup in the corrals, the men caught and threw calves, but Grandpa was the one who knew how to castrate them and notch their ears. He was also the cattle doctor, shoving pills down calves' throats with a metal tube and rubbing salt in the eyes of those with pink eye. Similarly with sheep. The men caught and held the lambs until he doctored them or, during the slaughter, cut their throats. My job in a cattle roundup was to tend the branding irons and keep them hot in the open-pit fire. Because I was a country kid I didn't have to go to kindergarten, and I remember thinking how happy I was to be out working on a cattle roundup with my grandpa and dad rather than being in school.

When I was ten, I stood behind my mother inside the house and heard her telling Grandpa through the screen door that his eighty-four-year-old mother had just died in L.A. He stood on the porch in bright sunlight on the other side of the screen, nodded, turned, and walked away, leaving me to think, for better or worse, this is how a man responds to grief.

The evening after all his teeth were pulled for dentures, I went out to the garden to pick rosemary and thyme for dinner and saw him spitting blood into the dirt. He looked up at me, stopped spitting, and asked about dinner. I never heard him complain. We went inside and, as usual, before dinner, he let me take a sip of his Old Fashioned.

For all the stories I heard about my grandfather, the only time I saw him truly angry was one raw November evening—it was already dark—when he stood on a cotton wagon and yelled down at the guy in charge of the crew who had picked the cotton. I couldn't understand Spanish, but I knew the cotton was dirty, mixed with boles, clods, and leaves, and my grandfather, outlined against the starry sky, hollered in rapid-fire Spanish and angrily threw great clouds of cotton off the wagon into the night air.

One time he slapped me, not hard, but quickly when I was throwing a fit in front of my mother during an argument we were having after we'd dressed up to go out to dinner. She told me to tuck in the red bandana I insisted on dangling from my back pocket. The unexpected slap and order, "Pipe down," shocked me as a particularly stinging injustice because, as I was trying to explain to my mother, I wanted my handkerchief to hang down

out of my back pocket exactly the way Grandpa's did during
the day, a red cowboy handkerchief from Levi's we both got at
the Money Back Sam men's store. Just as I was about to cry, he
reached into his pocket and said, "Here," handing me a quarter,
and I felt immediately better. He was making up. A quarter was
a lot of money in those days.

Another time, at a spring school fundraiser in the parish hall,
I won a lamb in a raffle. Although I was only a kid and people
were telling me how my family would enjoy this lamb at Easter,
my grandfather made no such assumption. He recognized it
as my lamb and made a deal to buy it from me, which struck
me even at the time as characteristic of his sense of reciproc-
ity. Of course, he got a good price. I watched him work at the
big wooden butcher block in his shop, carve off a leg of lamb
for Easter dinner, and package the rest for the freezer. From
him, I learned how to kill and pluck chickens and dress doves,
quail, pheasants, and ducks. In the fall, he moved outside his
butcher shop to salt down the cavity of a deer carcass, hanging
from a sycamore. He was the one who gave me my first gun, a
single-shot .410 shotgun, and took me out the next morning for
a ritualistic shooting lesson, which was perfunctory. I'd already
been to gun-safety classes. He pointed to a bird on a distant wire.
"Shoot that bird," he said. He watched me load, aim, and shoot.
He nodded. That was it.

When I was nine he went to Béarn to visit relatives and sent
me a postcard showing the torero Antonio Ordóñez caping a
fighting bull with big horns in a close *pase en rondo*. "You see
this is a bad looking bull," my grandfather wrote on the back of
the card, going on to advise me to "when you go around in those
pastures look out for the bulls. I hope you are helping your dad
with the work on the ranch." He himself had shot a rabbit that
morning outside Oloron-Sainte-Marie and was "going to hunt

wild boar on Sunday." He would be home before long and hoped I was being a good boy.

His card explicitly underscored lessons he implicitly taught. Ranch life could be dangerous and you needed to know what to do ("watch out for those bulls"). I had seen him and my dad ride out to break up two bulls fighting in a pasture, but I wasn't there to see how they'd done it, though I'd later seen the bleeding bulls. It wasn't school tasks he urged on me as a good boy, but "work on the ranch," implying perhaps that helping my dad extended beyond my earlier chores from the age of five to water tomatoes and beans in the garden, feed the chickens, gather the eggs, empty the garbage, burn the trash, and so forth. And when not working the most gratifying and useful recreation I could do was "going to hunt," mostly things to eat but on occasion pests.

What the card didn't tell me was the deep connection my grandfather felt for the people he was visiting in France when he wrote me. To me Grandpa was a California-born American, an iconic Western rancher. I didn't comprehend at the time how much his Béarnais heritage had shaped him; his parents were immigrants, his wife Anna was an immigrant, his California aunts, uncles, and cousins were immigrants. He grew up in a vibrant Los Angeles community of Béarnais immigrants. He worked and partnered in the San Joaquin Valley with Béarnais and Basque farmers from the Pyrenees.

Years later in Oloron, I met Prosper's Béarnais cousin Urbain Davancens—their mothers were sisters. Urbain and his wife, Marie-Louise Lasserre-Davancens, had been resisters during the Second World War and were sent to Nazi prison camps. Marie-Louise was Basque and until she was five spoke only Basque before learning French in school. She recalled the incarceration with her mother at Ravensbrück: "Our hut was next to the crematory ovens. Day after day, we smelled the unbearable smell of burned flesh." When American and Russian troops liberated the camp, Marie-Louise weighed sixty pounds. She and her mother were the only survivors from their village. She nevertheless at no time ever regretted helping the Resistance.

Twenty years after I met her, Marie-Louise revealed these prison details in recorded and written accounts that I read in Sandra Ott's *War, Judgment, and Memory in the Basque Borderlands, 1914–1945*. My cousin Marc Davancens, an architect in Oloron, later sent me documents of Urbain's arrest by the Waffen-SS and his imprisonment. I had no idea about my relatives' wartime experiences, but my grandfather did. He knew that Urbain and Marie-Louise had met and married after the war, but the only mention Marie-Louise and Urbain made to me about the war was to say that after they returned home as former German POWs they had nothing. When my wife, Holly, and I visited, they owned a boucherie charcuterie in Oloron-Sainte-Marie next to the house where we ate lunch, but despite their own success and prosperity they wanted to talk about Prosper. They admired his fluency in French. Urbain said that one morning he and some family members were speaking privately when Prosper walked in and surprised everyone by saying, "I know what you're saying," and began speaking to them in perfect Béarnais. Urbain fixated on Prosper's success as a rancher and kept asking me specific questions about his tractors and other machinery. Several relatives extolled Prosper's prowess as a hunter. Urbain, himself a famed hunter and guide in the Pyrenees, said, "He was such a good shot." When they all went duck hunting, Urbain said, everyone regularly missed except Prosper. He would shoot three ducks, which was the limit, and give them to someone who had none, then shoot three more.

Besides serving for me as a model hunter, my grandfather also gave me one of my earliest lessons in aesthetics. We went into town together to a hall where two sportsmen gave talks and showed movies, one of a big-game safari, the other of an Alaskan salmon-fishing trip. "Which did you like better?" he asked me afterward. I thought the answer was obvious. The African film about lions and rhinoceroses was clearly more dramatic and exciting than the one about a few grizzlies and a bunch of fish. To my surprise, he liked the Alaskan film. After he explained how we learned fresh things from the Alaskan fisherman, I realized my initial response to the safari was to clichés and stereotypes we'd already encountered in his *National Geographic*s and in the photos of his zebra-striped edition of Osa Johnson's *I Married Adventure*.

The particular affection I felt for my grandfather certainly conforms to the truism about how genetic affinities skip a generation. Grandparents and grandchildren often form more familial bonds, or at least less sullied ones, than those between parents and children. In his back bedroom, my grandfather and I slept together in the same bed when my family moved into the ranch house with him after the Second World War. "Go warm up the bed," Grandpa said every night when it was time. It seemed I was usually asleep when he came to bed, though sometimes I saw him taking off his Levi's before getting into bed in his long johns.

On the wall above our heads, we slept under an inexpensive gilt-framed painting of cows in a pastoral valley along a shallow river under sloping hills. This photomechanical reproduction now hangs in the study where I'm writing. The painting at first looks more like a nineteenth-century Hudson Valley scene by Asher Durand than it does like California, but a second look suggests the scene is French, though for me it evokes a pastoral California that is gone. I think of my grandfather, my dad, and my grandmother picnicking by the San Joaquin River and stringing mushrooms. I look at the painting and think of the mornings my grandfather woke me before dawn for a roundup, when we rode horseback along Cottonwood Creek to gather cattle. I wonder what visions of ranching sustained him from when he was a young tenant farmer in Los Angeles until he acquired his own land and became the Old Man in the San Joaquin Valley. I never got a sense that all he wanted was money. I like to think he hung this painting above his bed because its pastoral vision could belong in the West as well as the Barétous Valley, where his ancestors had farmed and his mother, Marie Jeanne, and his wife, Anna, were born, a vision that nourished both his life and work.

When he was seventy, he remarried, driving to Las Vegas to do so, and moved into town to use indoor plumbing for the first time. The outhouse he used on the ranch when I lived with him was removed and the pit covered up.

We were all back at the ranch on an April evening to celebrate his seventy-third birthday. After dinner, we started to watch slides when someone said, "Something's wrong with Pop." He was having a heart attack. I rode with him stretched out in the back of the station wagon, and having recently learned mouth-to-mouth resuscitation, I put my mouth to his. The tip of his tongue slid forward to touch my tongue, and I knew he was dead.

When we arrived at the hospital, Old Doctor Butler pulled his car up to the curb and started walking across the street toward us.

"Hurry, doctor," my aunt said.

The old doctor didn't hurry. He continued walking slowly across the dark street and came into view under the streetlights. He reached into the back of the station wagon, held my grandfather's wrist, and pulled his hand away.

"Is he dead, doctor?" my aunt asked.

"Oh, yes," Doctor Butler said. "Pop's gone."

Reading Steinbeck

John Steinbeck was my favorite writer in my teens, the one most connected to the California ranch life I knew. I must admit I've avoided rereading him since those years, even when I had occasion to teach classes or to direct student theses on Steinbeck's work. Once, after students in my seminar elected to read *The Grapes of Wrath*, the poet Philip Levine, who'd come from the San Joaquin Valley as the visiting writer in residence at my college, agreed to lead the discussion of this novel he knew so well. "I've not only taught the novel," Philip Levine told me, "I've taught it to the children of *The Grapes of Wrath*." I was off the hook, but on my own I would have felt comfortable drawing from memory. That memory, burned into my awareness at a young age, leads me to pay homage to the Steinbeck of my boyhood because my youthful reading of his fiction about the Salinas Valley made me see ranch country in a new way. At the same time, I faced a conflicting realization of how he'd misunderstood and misrepresented the valley where I lived.

From friends and relatives I continue to hear complaints, how the rural San Joaquin Valley and its small towns get a bum rap. Or no rap at all. A common refrain arises: "It's like we don't exist. We're invisible." Drive-by reports by eastern journalists today foster a widespread sense among valley residents of being either ignored or maligned. In response, valley-born novelist Manuel Muñoz recently said, "I write about the Central Valley because it remains a strangely unexplored area of our nation. As a region, it gives so much of its bounty to the rest of the country and receives little in return."

As a boy, I knew nothing about the historical misrepresentations of Steinbeck and others. I remember the afternoon on my family's San Joaquin Valley ranch when I was reading my first Steinbeck novel, *Of Mice and Men*, and saw a description of water rippling over yellow sand much like that in the irrigation ditch I could see through the window across the road. For the first time I encountered in a book a commonplace of my daily experience. I looked from the novel to the ditch and the field beyond. Outside became inside, inside outside. I saw as if in a jolt of light the ordinary surroundings of my life become worthy of literature.

I then went on to read almost all of Steinbeck's novels and stories. I recall his visions of fields and wind and dust, the gang plows that turned up the black soil, the lupine with petals edged in white, and the California poppies the color of cream as if skimmed from liquefied gold—an image forever imprinted on my brain. A playmate's mother, seeing me read a Steinbeck novel, asked if I thought there could be in real life such a wicked woman as his fictional character Cathy Ames. I said yes. What did I know? This discovery of sexual mysteries in literature coincided with my own, and it was all a shimmering confusion. A man in a Steinbeck novel who wore a glove to keep his hand soft for his wife merely hinted at what I was learning from ranch hands and fieldworkers during the summers.

As I sat in a boarding school classroom on the California coast, I daydreamed often of those men and women, the way they worked, the injustices they experienced, the dignity they showed. I wanted to be out in the fields with them rather than at my desk. Coincident with those daydreams was one of John Steinbeck stopping for me on Highway 101 as I hitchhiked between ranch and school. Not an impossible reverie. He must drive that road a lot, I thought; it runs right through the Salinas Valley. Our affinity would allow us to talk. He knew things, such as the way a working man blows his nose onto the ground, first through one nostril, then the other, while pinching the opposite shut with a thumb, like the buckaroo in *The Red Pony*—and like my dad and granddad. He knew that rain and sunlight and fog were more than a region's weather; they reflected its moods, expressed its soul. What I couldn't articulate at the time was that Steinbeck's fiction proclaimed what I wasn't learning in school: the ethnically rich valleys and foothills of the agricultural West, the fields and their workers, the drifters and outcasts—indeed, their ways of life—were important.

When I was asked to write a college freshman essay on my hometown, I titled it "Between Lennie and Aram" to describe the hodgepodge, immigrant-filled, Western-tinged overlap of John Steinbeck's fields and William Saroyan's vineyards that I felt largely defined the irrigated expanse of the San Joaquin Valley. Aram was Armenian, born of immigrant parents twenty-five miles south of my grandfather's ranch. Lennie arrived later, one of nearly a million generically labeled "Okies" who began migrating to California early in the twentieth century, mainly from Oklahoma, Texas, Arkansas, and Missouri, as well as other midwestern and southern states, with most arriving as so-called Dust Bowl refugees during the Great Depression.

Steinbeck highlighted labor struggles that had long defined the working-class valley. According to San Francisco's *Daily Morning Chronicle*, "The farm labor problem of California is undoubtedly the worst in the United States." That was in 1875. Many valley farm laborers were then Chinese, former gold miners, railroad builders, and even strikers who'd demanded a twelve-hour day and forty dollars a month from the Central Pacific. Fifty-five years later during the Great Depression, eight thousand Chinese, Japanese, Filipino, Mexican, and Punjabi farmworkers went on strike in the Imperial Valley. Three years later, ten thousand San Joaquin Valley cotton pickers began the biggest farm strike in the country's history. That was in 1933. Six years later, strikebreakers with pick handles and rubber hoses attacked a cotton workers' meeting in the courthouse park of my hometown of Madera. After 180 agricultural strikes, Governor Culbert Olson appointed Carey McWilliams to lead the first farm wage-rate hearings in California's history, which also took place in Madera, because that's where a recent surge of Okie migrants had doubled the county's population.

Labor historian Frank Bardacke, who for ten years worked in the fields himself, objects to widespread images in popular culture of suffering and defeated farmworkers as an insult to their tradition of fighting back and even winning. In his powerful history *Trampling Out the Vintage*, he notes how twenty-one of the twenty-five strikes in 1933 increased farmworkers' pay, though wages plummeted again at the end of the decade with reduced cotton acreage, too many workers, and not enough jobs. As a boy when I'd read *In Dubious Battle*, I hadn't known how Steinbeck had altered history. Strikers were crushed in Steinbeck's novel, but peach pickers won the actual strike that inspired his story. Steinbeck would live long enough to see Filipino and Mexican workers launch the Delano table-grape strike and boycott, but not to see lettuce harvesters in his own Salinas Valley in 1976 lead the most successful farmworkers' strike in U.S. history.

The Grapes of Wrath was published in 1939, the same year as Carey McWilliams's *Factories in the Field*, a book claiming that the division between fields and factories was artificial. "The distinction between farm and city is practically meaningless today," McWilliams wrote, something I had a hard time seeing even twenty-five years later. The book's title eloquently spoke to the power of metaphor, but I agreed with Bardacke that McWilliams's "wonderful, albeit misleading, title" created much confusion. I also tended to side with the *San Francisco Chronicle* writer and union activist Stephen Suleyman Schwartz, who called McWilliams's claim "a breath-taking flight of sociological hallucination."

In the context of the 1930s, it's necessary to appreciate the outrage of Steinbeck and McWilliams at the suffering and injustice experienced by migrant workers. The writers felt a need to shout at public indifference to a massive social crisis. Two years after the San Joaquin Valley cotton strikes, McWilliams took a trip to find out what was going on: "In the summer of 1935, in company with Herbert Klein," he wrote, "I made a trip through the San Joaquin Valley, inspecting some of the ranches, talking with workers, interviewing organizers who had been active in the strikes of 1933." After a twelve-day tour in May with his fellow journalist that included visits to Sacramento and Salinas as well as Bakersfield and Fresno, McWilliams returned to Los Angeles to write six pieces for the *Pacific Weekly*, later expanded into his best-selling work. He didn't mention *The Grapes of Wrath*, he explained to readers, because he'd submitted his final manuscript to publishers before the publication of Steinbeck's "excellent book."

Steinbeck and McWilliams believed California land barons created "fascist control" (McWilliams) over "our own highly organized industrial farming" (Steinbeck). Both men connected these feudal empires to the heyday of big wheat ranches portrayed in Frank Norris's *The Octopus: A Story of California*. Published in 1901, Norris's novel presented the first powerful literary description of mechanized ranches in the San Joaquin Valley, "ruled with iron and steam" through gigantic gang plows and combine harvesters capable of reaping, threshing, and winnowing wheat. Norris's main point was that the biggest California landowner wasn't a rancher or farmer but the Southern Pacific Railroad— the "Octopus"—its tentacles grabbing millions of acres.

What McWilliams doesn't say, or didn't know, was that in 1899 when Frank Norris made a brief visit to the San Joaquin Valley the big wheat ranches he was looking for had vanished, replaced in part by the smaller orchards and vineyards Steinbeck's migrating Okies would glimpse from the Tehachapi mountains some forty years later as they drove into the valley. In his novel, Norris created the landscape he wanted by moving a Spanish mission, a Mexican town, and a large fictitious Mexican rancho, bestowed "from the Spanish crown," over the Coast Range into the San Joaquin Valley to foster an ongoing myth of how Spanish and Mexican settlements morphed into the valley's immense wheat and cattle ranches that monopolized the land.

To understand the exploitation of California farm labor, McWilliams incorrectly explained how the monopolistic character of San Joaquin Valley ownership extends back to Spanish and Mexican land grants. His point about these estates is that they weren't broken up. "The vast feudal holdings," he mistakenly wrote, "were never disrupted." Even in 1860, McWilliams claimed, ten years after statehood, the prospective California farmer in almost every direction ran into a Mexican land grant. "The ownership changed from Mexican grantee to American capitalist," he wrote. "The most remarkable single circumstance pertaining to the entire record is the unbroken continuity of control."

The problem here is that McWilliams gets his history all wrong. There were no Spanish land grants in the Central Valley. Under the subsequent twenty-year Mexican rule, there were no settled ranchos in the San Joaquin Valley. California rancheros, uninterested in the interior valleys, settled on the fertile coast. Among some 450 Mexican land grants, most of them hurriedly dispensed during the last six years of the Mexican era as protection against American invasion, only ten were in the San

Joaquin Valley. Like many quickly issued grants they remained undeveloped on the ground and designated only on paper with such vague boundary points as "a large oak with cut branches" or "the place where Don Simeon Castro sits on his white horse each evening." After 1850, most Mexican grants throughout the state were broken up, sold, or unpatented.

Neither Steinbeck nor McWilliams was a historian, and like Norris neither spent much time in the valley, but their views of large-scale industrial land monopoly continue to influence historical writing about the valley. Patricia Limerick, a leading advocate for what was labeled the New Western History, amplifies misinformation about the valley in *The Legacy of Conquest: The Unbroken Past of the American West*. She presents a common view of the California myth that tends to parrot McWilliams in a simplified description of nineteenth-century agriculture, "when," as Limerick writes, "large-scale wheat ranching appeared in the Central Valley, in California." She goes on to explain: "There estates from the Spanish and Mexican era set a pattern of large-scale land holding. The economy of scale required by certain kinds of irrigation confirmed the pattern. Large-scale farming, rechristened agribusiness, dominated California farming, relying on seasonal migrant labor of varying nationalities—men and women representing the exact opposite of the Jeffersonian agrarian ideal. In the twentieth century, the rest of the West leaned toward California's pattern."

Limerick here follows McWilliams, who in turn followed the earlier journalist and political economist Henry George in his 1871 report, *Our Land and Land Policy*. This practice demonstrates the limitations of writing history driven by ideology rather than research. Some recent historians offer corrections. Lisbeth Haas in *Conquests and Historical Identities in California, 1769–1936* sums up how California law allowed squatters to seize uncultivated land of unconfirmed ranchos. Even those large Mexican estates approved after the California Land Act of 1851 were then legally divided at a rapid pace. "In the relatively cash-scarce economy of California," Haas writes, "lawyers, land speculators, surveyors, new immigrants with ready cash, and squatters ended up owning or claiming all or portions of almost every ranch in the state."

One of those Mexican estates was Rancho La Brea in Los Angeles, where my great-grandfather was a tenant farmer for the family of Henry Hancock, the lawyer who acquired the property as legal payment from the original Mexican owners, who went broke during years of rightfully proving their claim in U.S. courts. The land was then broken up.

Here's what happened in the valley where I grew up. The only Mexican land grant in Madera County disappeared when U.S. courts failed to validate it. After the annihilation of valley Indians and the devastating floods and drought of 1861–1864, government largess allowed the San Francisco speculators Isaac Friedlander and William Chapman and the cattleman Henry Miller, all immigrants, to buy or claim hundreds of thousands of acres of public land. That's half the story. The other half is that Miller tried to keep his land while the two speculators broke their holdings into tracts. They sold one tract along Cottonwood Creek, two miles east of my family's future ranch, called the Alabama Colony, to former Confederate plantation owners, charging double the $1.25 per acre the speculators had paid to the U.S. Land Office. Other real estate was sold and broken into the twenty-acre farms of the Central California Colony south of Fresno. In 1876, Friedlander gave forty acres of raw land to form the terminal of the Madera logging flume and my future hometown in exchange for flume water for irrigation. The John Brown Colony, south of Cottonwood Creek and a mile from the ranch where I would later grow up, consisted of 3,500 acres divided into five-acre farms and a town called La Vina with some thirty houses, a post office, a grocery store, a bank, two churches, a saloon, and a two-story schoolhouse with fifty-two students and two teachers, until everything collapsed in the farming depression of the 1890s.

"Settlers from Norway, Sweden, Denmark, England, Germany, Portugal, Italy, Turkish Armenia, Russia, China, and Japan came to Fresno during the 1880s and 1890s," David Vaught writes in his revealing book, *Cultivating California: Growers, Specialty Crops, and Labor, 1875–1920.* The center of the San Joaquin Valley "became one of the more cosmopolitan regions in the country." By 1900, farming colonies blurred into new settlements, "creating a vast, unbroken region of small farmers."

Most published works of California farm labor history, as Vaught documents, follow the "factories in the field" paradigm established by Carey McWilliams eighty years ago. McWilliams focuses on the anomalous history of the Miller & Lux cattle company as a typical industrial agribusiness. He presents an equally distorted account of "the Wheatland Riot" as the central labor event in California's agricultural history. "McWilliams sought to create a usable past to explain his disturbing present," Vaught writes, "but at the cost of trying to see the past as it actually happened." The valley had both big and small farms, many family-owned, but California farms and ranches were then smaller on average than in the rest of the country, as they are today.

Thirteen years after publishing his novel, Steinbeck told *Voice of America*, "When I wrote *The Grapes of Wrath*, I was filled, naturally, with certain angers—certain angers at people who were doing injustices to other people—or so I thought. I realize now everyone was caught in the same trap. If you remember we had a depression at the time. The Depression caught us without the ability to take care of it."

During that Depression, when McWilliams drove through the San Joaquin Valley, he didn't return with any firsthand observations of farmers or workers for his book. *Factories in the Field* presents a view from the highway. McWilliams notes how travelers "gaze upon vast tracts of farm land stretching away on either side of the road." He projects an imaginary farm scene: "In the harvest seasons, the orchards are peopled with thousands of workers, and, in the great fields, an army of pickers can be seen trudging along, in the dazzling heat, in the wake of a machine," though it's unclear what kind of machine and harvest he might be imagining. "Occasionally the highway passes within a view of barracklike shacks," he writes, and "huge orchard and garden estates, without permanent occupants." He wonders, "Where are the farmers? Where are farmhouses?"

We were there. Or my family was. Off the highway. Although predictive of future mechanization, McWilliams's metaphoric image of immense corporate industrial farms obscured the valley's many family farms and the workers whose hands picked the cotton, grapes, apricots, olives, peaches, tomatoes, and other crops.

In Steinbeck's fiction, for all the attention he gives to valley farm laborers, scenes of actual work are missing from his pages. They later turned up in Leonard Gardner's novel, *Fat City*, where African Americans, Filipinos, Mexicans, and Okies come together in valley fields, boxing gyms, and skid-row bars as simultaneous Western dreamers and losers. They live on the edge of a receding older West and an advancing new one, site of the true West, as always, a place where memories of past glory and loss fade into dreams of the future. The true West dreamer-loser phenomenon also persists in the post-Steinbeck, working-class California of Gerald Haslam's fiction, Wilma Elizabeth McDaniel's poems, Sam Shepard's plays, Ron Hughart's memoirs, and Merle Haggard's songs.

Close to the valley life I knew, an hour and a half north of where I grew up, was Riverbank, the boyhood home of Oscar Zeta Acosta, author of *Autobiography of a Brown Buffalo*. Riverbank was only a few minutes from Modesto, the setting of George Lucas's *American Graffiti*, a movie actually filmed for the most part near the coast in Petaluma but still an iconic rendition of small-town Central Valley life to many Californians. Acosta's Riverbank feels truer, more like the California valley towns of my boyhood that the critic Richard Gilman describes as the "psychic and imaginative ground" of Sam Shepard's plays, "a life resembling that in the movie *American Graffiti*, only tougher, shrewder, more seeded with intimations of catastrophe." Acosta's experience defines the California dream of the San Joaquin Valley in true West fashion as one of aspiration and defeat, hope and disappointment, optimistic longing and sobering failure. The dreams and losses go on in contemporary California with Chicanos and Chicanas in the writings of Dagoberto Gilb, Richard Rodríguez, Floyd Salas, Helena María Viramontes, Gary Soto, Juan Felipe Herrera, Luis Valdez, Josefina López, José Montoya, Tim Z. Hernandez, Manuel Muñoz, Lorna Dee Cervantes, and others you can read in *Huizache: The Magazine of Latino Literature*.

The persistence of the California dream in the San Joaquin Valley came home to me when my boyhood valley friend Chris emailed from Oregon about her sense of herself as a Californian and Westerner. "I've just received," she wrote, "carefully labeled photos of the graves of all my Westering California ancestors in the Madera Arbor Vitae cemetery. They are lined up on two sides of the family with births dating back to 1807. As I look at them I'm certain that I am a Californian, not just an Oregonian transplant, and certain that I'm part of the Western tradition. California is not just ethnic diversity and geography; it's a freedom of spirit, which is the essence of the West that allows for excesses and major mistakes, both environmental and personal—tending to self-destruction in our small worldview. I'm sure I'm part of that as I watch my children walk on stilts to other geographical reaches beyond the Central Valley, never to return to that family graveyard as burned-up symbols of the Western freedom of spirit. I am comfortable with the California Western myth and tradition, knowing that I, too, can, if I choose, burn out my spirit or make it glow."

Why then haven't I gone back to Steinbeck's books? I count sixteen hardbacks on my shelves. I partly fear not finding what was once there. I had occasion not long ago to look through *Of Mice and Men* but couldn't locate the startling image of irrigation water as I remembered it. I now see it was in *East of Eden*. I don't want to reread either novel to discover what I might perceive as sentimentality and caricatures to sully my boyhood memory of those fictional worlds. The other reason I haven't reread him is that until recently I hadn't wanted to think or write about my boyhood and the jumble of memories from my own experience that are so intertwined with those of reading Steinbeck's fiction. The coming-of-age story, often a novelist's first subject, seemed to me the most difficult. I wanted time and practice before attempting it, as I finally did in my fourth novel, *Jesse's Ghost*.

I recall liking best some of Steinbeck's stories in *The Pastures of Heaven* and *The Long Valley*. From my bookshelf, I pull out *The Long Valley*. There it is on the first page: the land after the bustle of the fall harvest, the gang plows leaving the black earth shining like metal where the shares had cut, the yellow stubble fields, the pale cold sunshine on the foothills, the fog covering the valley like a closed pot, "a time of quiet and waiting," as Steinbeck describes it. Both land and people need to pause. Then the moment arrives to go on. It's all there. I think I'll keep going on.

Seeing the Mountains

Mornings on the ranch when I was a boy began along the eastern horizon with the heart-lifting apparition of the snowy Sierra Nevada—"the Range of Light," as John Muir called it—and evenings closed with sundowns behind the lavender Diablo Range, and I knew I lived in the Great Valley. I ended up in valleys much of my life, cradled between mountains whose contrasting wildness and mystery give meaning to the pastoral domesticity along lower river bottoms. The Hudson Valley, where I spent most of my professional life in a house on the west bank of the river, rises into the haunted Catskills, a region spooky enough for a man named Rip to fall asleep for twenty years. The Jobal Valley in Chiapas, where I wrote the bulk of three novels, looks up into the mountains of Maya Indians and Zapatista rebels. Even my home in Blanco Basin—a no-exit valley—dead-ends against what was once the last wild abode of Colorado grizzlies. In the mountains we feel free, declares a character in T. S. Eliot's *The Waste Land*, and as a boy in the San Joaquin Valley, the ability to see the mountains reminded me, at least, of the mythic freedom of the West.

Below in the valley we were meant to be dutiful, mostly toilers in the earth, early to bed after brushing (we didn't floss in those days) and early to rise with my combed wet hair frozen stiff on cold February mornings while I waited along the road in the fog for the school bus. Wildness in the valley took both destructive forms of heavy drinking and overeating and the controlled violence of sports, especially high school boxing, wrestling, and football, but in the mountains what was otherwise forbidden became okay. In grade school, I was given a priestly dispensation to miss Sunday mass in order to spend the weekend in the mountains with a friend and his family who were horse outfitters and wranglers, a violation of ecclesiastical law I found troubling at the time, but less so as I realized that mountains possessed their own rules and spiritual rewards.

The mountains were the remote refuge where I saddled up with two high school friends and packhorses to fish for golden trout and to soothe a hurt heart. Weekends in high school found us taking a six-pack drive up to Ducey's Bass Lake Lodge, a place for fistfighting and for dancing to Eddie and the Rebels or Ray Camacho and the Teardrops. California motorcycle gangs like the Hell's Angels, Satan's Slaves, and Devil's Disciples mixed with us during their summer rally in the mountains at Bass Lake. In the valley, I hunted quail, doves, pheasants, ducks, rabbits, and other small game, but it was from the nearby and distant mountainous West that my grandfather brought back big game— mule deer, pronghorn, moose, and elk.

We were lucky, I think, in what the Boy Scouts offered us, the chance to camp and hike and fish with valley men who took the time to go into the mountains with us, untouched, at least to my knowledge, by scandals made known elsewhere in later years. We saw ourselves in the tradition of mountain men, making our way through the wilderness. In the high peaks we benightedly looked down our noses at backpacking Sierra Clubbers who used propane canisters to cook, while we chopped wood and built fires in accord with our notions of the authentic old days. We felt our own purblind superiority as we literally looked down from *our* mountains into Yosemite Valley at what we considered to be wimpy tourists in cabins or trailers. "I think," our scoutmaster told us, "Madera County has the finest mountains in California."

In any event, they were the wildest, we thought, the least trod, with clear lakes above the timberline, mostly free of other campers and hikers. As Boy Scouts and Explorer Scouts, we mixed among ourselves to an even greater degree than already allowed in the socially porous valley town we came from. While a black boy had never slept over at my house, or I at his, we became pup-tent mates on a Boy Scout camping trip in the mountains. Away from valley supervision, we were also suspected of misbehaving even when we weren't. One afternoon a friend and I retreated to our tent to read, eliciting the certainty from one of our leaders, we later learned, that we'd stockpiled girly magazines into our packs, when, in fact we were reading novels; mine was Jack London's *Martin Eden*, and I wanted to finish it that day—never to forget the novel's final lines describing the eponymous hero's suicide when he knew he "had fallen into darkness. And at the instant he knew, he ceased to know."

In the mountains a suicide could seem noble, while the valley suicide of a boyhood friend, the alcoholism of our parents, and car crashes in the early morning darkness were shameful violations of domestic order not to be talked about, though their frequency threatened our powers of suppression. Before we could go to bars, a therapeutic release, allowing us to hoot, scream, and stomp our feet in public, occurred at professional wrestling matches in the Fresno Auditorium. Real wrestling was a big deal in the valley, and Madera High spawned Northern California champions who surpassed football players as our grade-school sports heroes. Professional wrestlers, though, transcended the humdrum reality of our everyday lives by combining fakery with athleticism to provide mythic drama. On Saturday nights, professional wrestling became our Passion Play, Fresno our Oberammergau.

There were good guys and bad guys, of course, as in the Passion Play, but it didn't matter to us who was who, or which was which, as long as they were skilled. We cheered handsome Enrique Torres, a native Californian and a former accomplished amateur who knew how to wrestle, so smooth and quick in his moves—and dispassionate—as he roused the crowd to a frenzy with his dramatic drop kicks and flying head scissors. Enrique sometimes teamed up with a former college standout, indestructible Leo Nomellini, the San Francisco 49er football star and later Hall of Fame pro, who played both offense and defense, never missing a game in fourteen years, while also wrestling during the off-season. Truly a good guy, Leo the Lion responded in longhand when I later asked him to write something for my high school newspaper.

One of our favorites was a villain, Big Bill Miller, who'd defeated Leo Nomellini in college for the Big Ten heavyweight championship. I knew all these details from reading the wrestling magazines of the time. Dr. Bill, as he was sometimes called (he was a licensed veterinarian), made the Fresno auditorium shake with the crowd's rage as he taunted both his opponents and the audience with verbal abuse and every dastardly trick a dirty wrestler could muster, until he raised his foe into the air and finished him off across his knee with his notorious backbreaker. We loved him. Before Muhammad Ali, he was the greatest.

As I say, it didn't matter if a wrestler was a hero or a villain, cheered or booed, as long as he was accomplished, but it still came as a shock to me when I learned from my magazines that our California idol, Enrique Torres, was reviled in Texas as a villainous Mexican, "the Black Panther of Sonora." The lesson here—how nothing has meaning in itself but only in its environment—came home even stronger one day during lunch period at St. Joachim's School. My friends and I had prepared a program of pro wrestling after practicing on the grass to flip each other and bounce after landing on our backs, and to throw fake right crosses to the jaw. I laboriously typed up a program on my father's manual typewriter with a series of preliminary bouts and a main-event tag-team match in which I was one of the villains.

Our favorite teacher, the cherubic and peppy Sister Kathleen Mary, joined the crowd of pupils to cheer and jeer us on. As she and our schoolmates vociferously raged disapproval, with the good sister stomping her foot and booing me, I happily twisted my knuckles into my opponent's eye, while taunting onlookers, including the booing nun, with a malevolent grin and a shout, "Shut up!" An instant hush came over the yard. Sister Kathleen Mary blanched, waving her hands like a referee to bring the bout to a halt with the order "Stop." Rules of propriety instantly squashed the wild freedom of our play-acting. My fellow wrestlers and I were marched out of the schoolyard, back to the classrooms. Word went through the school that I'd told a nun to shut up. Although I suffered no other consequences except an admonition about showing respect to nuns and clergy, I was appalled by the ignorance of the religious, leaving me to think *Doesn't she know how the game is played? What we're doing and saying isn't real?*

The mountains harbored no such ignorance. Mountains allowed ritualized violations of valley probity. In the mountains we could pretend we were bad. At Camp Chawanakee on Shaver Lake, the outside walls of the big wooden dining hall of the Boy Scout summer camp displayed posters announcing our end-of-the-week tag-team wrestling match. Oversized cartoon figures of the wrestlers, drawn by a sweating adult family friend in our screened patio one hot summer afternoon at my urging, sort of looked like us, except that "Chief Kit Fox" was Richard Palacioz, one of the good guys, who would appear in the dirt ring wearing war paint and a full Plains Indian headdress. His partner, "Prince Miaropa" from India, was Mike Vizcarra, dressed in a turban and terrycloth robe meant to be royal. The referee who got into the action was Ronnie Preciado.

I was a villain—"Wild Bill Savage"—sporting a cowboy hat, a sky-blue neckerchief, and a handmade braided bullwhip given to me by a Béarnais-immigrant cowboy who'd worked on the King Ranch in Texas. My villainous partner was "Humpadink Hank" from the Ozarks, played by Eddie Palacioz, wearing a Hoss hat and drinking from an earthen jar of moonshine. Nattily dressed like an Old West bartender in black pants, black bow tie, black vest, and red shirt was the announcer, Paul Gonzalez.

In the weird light of the night's bonfire and surrounding torches, under stars and moon, for consecutive summers, we entertained troops of California scouts and their leaders. In an age without camcorders, no images would remain from our fantastical drama were it not for the grainy 16 mm film my father took of us rehearsing on the Bermuda grass in front of our ranch house. In the herky-jerky film, Richard Palacioz flies feet first into the air to hit me in the chin with a drop kick. Like Enrique Torres, he leaps up to hook his legs around my neck with a flying head scissors and flip me head over heels onto the grass. To my regret, that diminished rehearsal on film in no way reflects, through repeated practice, the act we managed to polish and perfect.

Our muted rehearsal became a frenzy on the nights of our performances in the mountains. My partner pretended to miss our enemy and accidentally slug me, and I, in turn, went nuts and attacked my partner. The hero Prince Miaropa went wild with right crosses to my jaw. I lifted the other hero, Chief Kit Fox, upside down next to the flames of the bonfire and repeatedly bounced his back into the dirt with merciless body slams. I tied the end of my twelve-foot bullwhip around his neck and flipped him again and again around the campfire ring at the end of the whip. He tried to run away toward our scoutmaster until the whip jerked him back and he flopped to the ground in a squirming heap, raising a fear in the crowd, that, indeed, as his partner screamed, his neck was broken.

The audience booed me in a rage, while I shook my fist, grinning maniacally. I screamed back at both scouts and our leaders, "Shut up." Their disapproval grew tumultuous. To be so vilified and so demonized—and, yes, so hated—filled me with electrifying joy. I heard the jeers as cheers for what I was doing so well, pretending to be bad, pretending to gouge out someone's eye, pretending to break the minimal rules of restraint imposed upon professional wrestling. The mob's intense emotion and my ability to generate it thrilled me beyond happiness. I was the one in control here, moving the crowd to heights of fury—or fake fury—because I wasn't really being bad. I was only pretending. It was all theater. It was all play-acting. And yet that fantasy released me of so much anger, guilt, and resentment I kept caged in the valley that I felt cleansed. I felt free. Without realizing it, I'd learned something about the cathartic powers of imaginative violence for the artist.

I also learned something about the effect of art on the audience that went against a cherished notion of Hollywood filmmakers. We, the villains, won, and we did it in the dirtiest manner possible—and though we were disqualified, we'd crushed the good guys—proving that happy endings are not what an audience necessarily desires, but only an experience both moving and meaningful, however dark.

With our Bakkheia terminated, our Walpurgisnacht behind us, our midsummer revels ended, we returned in September to assemble into obedient rows of pupils, the boys in salt-and-pepper cords and white shirts, the girls in white blouses with Peter Pan collars and navy blue skirts with straps, all in unison to pledge allegiance to the flag and to recite "The Apostles' Creed." In Lent, we marched to the Grotto, while singing "*O Maria, sine lave, conceptua...*" In the distant morning, I glimpsed the phantom range of light with its hints of wildness and freedom. Morning sightings of the snow-limned Sierra Nevada range made valley life beautiful.

But no more. The dirty, polluted sky has pretty much expunged a view of those spectacular, glistening mountains from our part of the valley, except on the occasion of a winter rain cleansing the air. Nothing to cry about, I'm told. Change is part of life, and pitiless extinction, especially of Western rural life, is an American given. Loss is common across the land, I know, but to my mind what is lost matters. In the San Joaquin Valley, we've lost the mountains.

Lina Mendive Bergon on horseback with her young son.

The Basque Nurse

Sometimes it's better to begin at the end, just to get it over with: my mother was sixty when she died of respiratory failure caused by acute alcohol poisoning. She'd been chugging gin and lay on the floor of her ranch house bedroom, tangled in sheets. The coroner reported that the alcohol level in her blood was .41 percent, more than killed the singer Amy Winehouse and more than five times the amount that would get you arrested today for drunk driving.

A happier image shows her on horseback in an old photograph from the mid-1940s. She was known as a Basque beauty. Dark-eyed, dark-haired in the photo, she stylishly wears a cowgirl neckerchief, a plaid shirt, embroidered leather riding gloves, and wide-legged Levi's with big cowboy cuffs. She holds the reins in her right hand and looks down at me on the saddle in front of her, about two years old, relaxed with my hand resting on the saddle horn and laughing at the camera. She's laughing, too, and we both look so happy.

How does one get from this bright beginning to the unhappy ending?

She was baptized Lina Rose Mendive, the second of eight children born to Basque immigrants in the high desert town of Battle Mountain, Nevada, where her parents ran a Basque hotel and grocery store for ranchers, miners, and sheepherders along the Union Pacific railroad tracks. She was the only one of the eight children to escape the sagebrush of Nevada at an early age, moving first to Salt Lake City after high school to become a registered nurse at Holy Cross Hospital and then to California, where in the romantic tradition of the lovers in *A Farewell to Arms* she nursed a patient in a Fresno hospital who later became her husband.

She was twenty-eight when she married, late for the times, but she was a woman with a career and previous beaus, handsome men next to her in photos, always in the stylish sports pants and dresses of the 1930s. Her husband, the son of a successful San Joaquin Valley rancher, was twenty-seven, a man with his own previous broken engagement but freshly graduated from the National Police Academy in Washington, D.C., when they married sixteen days later on July 22, 1940.

They were a handsome couple, although I hasten to say that when I was growing up beauty and money were two values never much remarked upon or pointed out in others. Only after hearing from others and from the hindsight of years do I see their good looks and joyful spirits in the photo of the young family seated on the concrete steps in front of the screen door and the asphalt siding of the modest apartment in Ely, Nevada, where we lived for a time during the Second World War and where I was born. My smiling father, in a suit and tie and the rimless glasses he wore like President Franklin Roosevelt, holds in a blanket my recently born baby sister, who looks to be howling.

My mother sits on the stoop in a 1940s straw boater with a decoratively veiled bumper brim and a shirtwaist dress with prominent buttons. What captures attention are both the happiness of her smile and her slender, eye-catching, crossed legs extending up from her pointed, open-toed shoes to a hemline barely covering her knees. I sit on the stoop next to her in a sailor suit of short pants and white shoes. My left hand rests on my mother's knee with the same easy casualness as it previously rested on the saddle horn when I rode with her horseback, but now I look warily at the camera.

As a California rancher's wife in the early 1950s, she could ride in roundups and knock down doves with a double-barrel shotgun.

A 16 mm film displays her at ease on horseback as she turns the horse past the camera. I'm now about six and not so happy riding behind her with my arms clasped tight around her waist during a phase in my life when after being bucked to the ground I'd grown afraid of horses. Her smile seems to reflect a bemusement at my fear, but I'm frightened and cling to her for safety.

When I was a child, although she no longer worked in the hospital, she practiced her profession on us. My sister recalls waking one night unable to breathe, blue with asthma, until my mother jabbed her arm with a hypodermic needle, injecting her with a shot of adrenaline. My sister felt cool air magically rush into her lungs.

As in many nurses' families, there was little sympathy in ours for ordinary sickness. When I contracted the mumps and chicken pox, which she diagnosed at the first symptoms, I got to stay home from school, but not when I broke my arm (I did get the afternoon off) or exhibited symptoms for colds. The only day in elementary school I recall skipping classes because of a cold was when the nuns called my mother to come and get me because I was coughing and sneezing too much in the classroom. Pink-and-white Benadryl capsules slid down our throats for sniffles and nearly every other discomfort, and they seemed to work because we believed they would work, though I now think she'd also found an efficient way to keep us sedated. In the bathroom she had a locked drawer full of syringes, gauzes, tapes, scissors, sutures, medicines, and sample drugs doctors gave her. I recall her twice bringing a sterilized needle close to my eyeball to pop a sty. We believed in what her medicaments and shots of penicillin could do, as well as enemas, my sisters tell me, which I don't recall, and so in grammar school I thought I made more ferocious tackles and stronger blocks during Saturday afternoon football games because she'd given me a shot in the arm of vitamin B.

The only time I saw her less than coolly matter-of-fact in her reaction to injury or illness was when at five I nearly cut off my finger with pruning shears. She started to cry as she held my dangling finger under the faucet of cold running water. The doctor took a chance on sewing me up and the finger was saved. I can still see the scar. Often she would sew up cuts on ranch workers unless they were deep and serious, as when my dad's foreman, Sonny, sliced his hand to the bone on a hay-mower sickle blade, and my mother calmly drove him to the hospital, he now recalls, as though she were out for a Sunday afternoon drive. "Come on, Lina," he said, "step on it," but she maintained her unhurried pace and casual conversation all the way to the hospital. I recall little sympathy for my father's bleeding ulcers and the operations to cure them, though he was able to stay on the couch in his den for a day after one operation.

Before we noticed her drinking I don't remember her ever being sick or staying in bed. I was in the seventh grade and we were in the family living room one evening, probably watching our first, newly arrived TV, when she stood up from her chair and began to cross the room as though teetering along a ledge with strange, tentative steps toward the hallway leading to her and my father's bedroom. Then she staggered. I responded in shock at what I interpreted as a display of the obvious. "She's drunk," I said aloud. My father jumped from his chair and rushed up behind her, saying, "No," in response to my accusation. He held her arms to steady her and guided her into the hallway and closed the door.

Flashes of meanness came with her drinking. She roughly pulled my sister's hair while braiding it, and my sister, who was in the fifth grade, said my mother would never touch her hair again, and she didn't. My sisters, brother, and I came to recognize the fractured gaze in her eyes that meant for the rest of the night she would be in a screaming rage until she conked out. If I shouted in anger for her to shut up, she would shout back, "I will not shut up until I am dead," repeating the refrain until the only recourse was to get the hell out. Better to tune out drunken

monologues and just shut down emotionally because confronta-
tions only generated accusations, such as "How can you love me
if you don't know me?" My father had several evening meetings,
almost certainly guaranteeing a rampage when he returned home
to perhaps not totally unjustified accusations such as "You didn't
marry me, you married the…" and here she would fill in the
name of the organization, hissing out the name of "the Elkssss"
or "the Knightssss." Even when I escaped to my bedroom, her
rages continued, sometimes outside the locked door. After I lay
in bed, waiting for peace, and finally falling asleep, I would jolt
awake to an eruption of renewed shouting. Many mornings I'd
find broken plates and glasses on the kitchen floor.

My mother's frightening volatility, my own angry responses
and subsequent shame, my simultaneous absence of feeling,
and my father's inability to protect us from her rage are here
summed up: "And when in the deep of night my mother came
into my room swaying, half conscious and with gray smoke from
her cigarette wreathing her face, shattered by bourbon and white
wine, and when she raised her hand to strike, and I easily batted
her arm back, then stepped forward and quickly steadied her
before she tipped; when, holding my mother upright, I looked
past her to see my father watching us from the shadows outside
my room, whispering that he was sorry for everything—when
these things happened, there eventually came a point at which
feeling, or whatever it is we call feeling, broke apart in me. And
though it's true that I felt anger and shame and fear—emotions
that I live with still…it was also true that I felt nothing at all."

Donald Antrim wrote these words about his mother in a
memoir called *The Afterlife*, published in 2006. I'm quoting
them here to point out what you already know from similar
stories you've heard or experienced yourself. In my story the
wine would be red, not white, and the bourbon would be gin, but

otherwise my memory differs little from Antrim's, right down to the gray cigarette smoke and the swaying, half-conscious face of my mother. The similarity is eerie. When I was a kid, I thought my experience was unique; now I know the tragedy of alcohol addiction is its dumb, predictable, but still widely unrecognized sameness.

When I drew details from my own mother's alcoholic behavior for a novel set in my boyhood hometown, one of my elementary school classmates, Jayne, wrote to me after reading it, "I thought maybe you took the ranting and raving part from my mom's behavior when she drank. I had no idea that others were going through the same trouble. I never would have guessed that your mother drank." Likewise, I hadn't known at the time that Jayne lived in a hellhole similar to mine.

The point I'm making here is how the horrific pattern of fractured alcoholic families is dismally undifferentiated. The drunken mother in Stephen Crane's 1893 masterpiece, *Maggie: A Girl of the Streets*, manages to encompass in expressionistic detail the same dreary psychological, verbal, and physical outrages of so many parents who lived secret and not-so-secret lives in the San Joaquin Valley when I was growing up. Differences are superficial. Whether demonic or moony, bellicose or amorous, lachrymose or comatose, alcoholics become stereotypes. What's similar is the tragic destruction of their distinctive selves. I watched it happen to my mother.

The problem is we didn't understand what was going on, and many of us still don't. Denial of alcohol addiction and dependency in our culture continues to be huge. "It's menopause," my father told us kids. "This is what lots of women go through." In apparent corroboration of this claim I overheard my mother advising another woman what to do about hot flashes.

"Your mother works hard all day," Donald Antrim's father told his children. "She's just tired. She's tired."

Donald shouted out, "She's not tired! She's an alcoholic." I shouted much the same thing. But who pays attention, as Antrim asks, to an unhappy teenager?

Drunkenness was shameful, a weakness, a moral failing afflicting skid-row bums, not good families in the San Joaquin Valley, so it wasn't talked about in those days, except in hush-hush, embarrassed ways. We were trapped in the thinking of our times to consider these "spells" caused by some other psychological and emotional disorder. Only after days as well as nights of increasing violence was my mother shuttled off to a Scotts Valley detox-and-rehab facility on the coast. My brother and younger sister sent her this handwritten note:

Dear Mommy
I am just ready to go to school. I hope you get well. I will pray for you every day because I love you very much. write to me. love, Mark

Dear Mommy,
How are you? We're all right. We're all praying for you so that you get well soon. Please write. love, Marie. God Bless You.

It did no good. She went back to rehab, the same place, a second time. And there, sober, she was soon helping with other patients. When my sister Michele went to visit, my mother sat at the rehab desk in her nurse's uniform, greeting visitors.

Back home, she resumed the cycle of drunkenness and withdrawal. Our entire lives revolved around her drinking. Or her not-drinking. Either way we were warily trapped in the rhythms of alcohol addiction. Would she be sober when I returned home from boarding school or college with a friend? Would we have Thanksgiving with my grandfather without the dinner scattered across the floor? Would the night pass without our being woken with her shouting rages? Would I not see my terrified younger brother in the doorway desperately pleading with my parents to stop this fighting, for our father to do something about it? Would blood not be on the floor when someone got cut with a kitchen knife? The answer was always no, no, no, no, no, and yet morning brought hope for the new day to be different—or maybe next week, or next month.

How could such an extreme way of living go on and on? Why was not something done to end it? A bizarrely strange thing happened after a disastrous binge. It was as if we were supposed to act as if nothing had happened. It was to be forgotten. My mother when temporarily sober was not the same woman who'd been on a binge. She even looked different; her face shed its old crazed look, dropped years, and resembled a younger mother we'd previously known. To begin berating her for what another woman had done—the other drunken woman she remembered nothing about—seemed unjust. Given her temporary sobriety and our stifled angry feelings toward her, her rages somehow came to seem our fault, due, perhaps, to our own lack of love for her. When I saw the film *The Three Faces of Eve* I was fourteen and thought Joanne Woodward's portrayal of a woman with multiple personalities provided a shocking revelation about my mother.

My elementary school friend, Jayne, was thirteen when "something snapped" in her mother, who was the city clerk, the first female elected to that civic position. Her mother started going to bars and drinking heavily. "When she came home," Jayne said, "she ranted and raved and even slapped me very hard in the face once (junior and senior years of high school were very difficult), I slapped her back in the same way since she wasn't my mother at that moment, but just an effing drunk, and she never touched me again."

The difference between before-and-after scenes in our house—between encounters with my real mother and (to borrow Jayne's term) the "effing drunk"—assumed insane Pinteresque disjunctions. The same transformation happened with Antrim's mother, a similarity I found uncanny in his description of how after a bender "we took our mother's lead, our mother who lit a morning cigarette, swallowed her coffee, and, without memory of herself in her darker form, went to the office." My mother didn't go to the office, but in the 1960s she astonishingly went back to work as a nurse. She requalified herself and boned up on all the new medications—the only thing that worried her was the proliferation of new drugs since she'd last practiced twenty-five years earlier—but confident of her ability to catch up, she headed to work in a white cap, white dress, and white shoes at the Madera County Hospital.

My practical, straight-talking, down-to-earth mother from the West, who rode horses and fired shotguns, differed in radical ways from Donald Antrim's artistic, visionary mother from the South—when they were both sober. That's the point. When drunk they lost their distinctive characteristics to share commonplace traits of an addictive personality, but when sober they shined as distinct individuals. My brother, Mark, recalls our mother at sundown driving him as a child to a country crossroads and pulling to the side of the road. "Wait," she said, and then as the sun started to sink, she announced, "Okay, here they come," and emerging from the field a procession of ring-necked pheasants strutted across the road, their red wattles and golden feathers iridescent in the dying sunlight.

"Your mother was sure a beautiful woman," Cousin Henry told me, "before she started having her spells." He never connected her "spells" to alcohol.

"I'll never forget," Cousin Eddie said, "how beautifully your mother sang 'The Tennessee Waltz.' I always think of her when I hear that song."

My sister Michele's childhood friend Kay remembers my mother's earthy advice during a women's discussion about not having sex with husbands during their periods: "Oh, no, girls," my mother advised them with a laugh, "you just put a towel on the bedsheet."

That same earthiness led my mother to bring each of my sisters at different times to the hospital delivery room to see for themselves how babies are born. "I swore at that time," Michele said, "that I would never have a baby."

My other sister, Marie, said that as a child she'd wanted to be a nurse, an aspiration that vanished after she stood behind the doctor while he delivered the second child of an unwed fifteen-year-old, a graphic lesson as well, she suspected, orchestrated by our mother. "I think she was trying to tell me not to fool around with boys or this is what would happen."

My sister's final abandonment of her wish to become a nurse occurred during another hospital visit when she saw a tube attached to a funnel go down the throat of a ravaged woman in her mid-forties, an attempted suicide. "They poured something into the funnel that went directly into her stomach, waited until she started heaving, then turned the funnel upside down over a plastic bucket. Stomach fluid and bits and pieces of more than forty aspirin poured out. Eeeeeuuuuuwwwww!"

A Jesuit who taught at the boarding school I attended drove from the coast to our ranch one summer and after visiting with my mother came to see me in the alfalfa field where I was irrigating. He'd been talking to my mother, he said, and asked me if I knew how brilliant she was. "She could have been a doctor or a lawyer or a professor," he told me. At that time I didn't care, too emotionally numb to assent, overwhelmed with memories of her drunkenness.

In October of 2012, I visited with Virginia Yturalde, who'd worked as a nurses' aide in the maternity ward when my mother went back to nursing in the 1960s. "She was a lovely lady," Virginia told me, "very nice, very knowledgeable. She took me under her wing. She kind of got me hooked on nursing." My mother taught Virginia how to prepare and shave a mother for delivery or a C-section, how to care for newborns, clean them up, weigh them, and make their formulas every morning. "I think about her a lot," Virginia said. "I really enjoyed working with her. I learned a lot from her. She was a very lovely lady, so slim and proper."

I mentioned how my mother had a drinking problem and I was amazed that she went back to nursing and was able to do it.

"She did have a problem," Virginia said. "A lot of times she came in woozy—a lot of times. I remember she'd be walking down the hall—she was a good walker—but, you know, she'd lift a leg and put it down carefully, and I'd think, *Oh, Lina, you're at it again.* But she was always a lady, a perfect lady."

It occurred quite a bit, Virginia said, and all the nurses knew. I asked what would happen then. Would she be sent home?

"No, no. She'd keep going, she'd work her eight hours. We all used to protect her," meaning, Virginia told me, "we'd watch her, but she never did anything wrong. We always knew she was okay. She knew exactly what she was doing. She was very smart." Virginia recalled how when a baby wasn't breathing, my mother said, "Don't worry, we'll take care of it." She tapped the baby's chest and it resumed breathing. "Keep an eye on it," she told Virginia, "and if it stops breathing again we'll call the doctor."

Virginia said. "You never had to worry about her making a boo-boo."

I asked why after a few years back at the hospital my mother had again stopped nursing, but Virginia didn't recall. Drugs weren't a problem. In their department they were in charge of labor and delivery as well as the nursery, and there weren't that many narcotics. "You could smell her when she first came in," Virginia said about my mother when she'd been drinking.

Virginia assured me, "There was no scandal or anything like that; otherwise, I would remember. Nobody could ever say anything wrong about Lina. She was always in charge, she always knew what she was doing."

I asked if the doctors at the hospital knew about her drinking. Virginia replied, "Oh, yes. All the doctors knew."

I could understand the nurses' silence as long as my mother, one of them, did her job, but I was surprised that doctors, aware of the situation, would let her continue to work. "Why didn't the doctors do something about it?" I asked.

"Because we all loved Lina," Virginia said.

This same woman—my mother—when drunk would yell at me nonstop, "I will not shut up until I'm dead and then I will haunt you.... *Mierda frita*...I could have strangled you when you were born....Think about it." Well, she had a point.

In portraying my mother in these extreme ways, I might be accused of avoiding a psychological connection between the two women I'm describing—after all I could cite instances of her temper and discontent in pre-drinking days, and her rages did give voice to some legitimate grievances unrelated to drinking—but the connection is small compared to the larger truth. Drinking can intertwine with emotional and psychological problems—and even create and exacerbate them—but those problems are not the causes of why she drank as she did. She was addicted. I have friends today who miss the point in probing only psychological or emotional causes for destructive drinking. Whenever I hear one of them musing about a relative and asking, "I wonder

what caused Uncle Joe to drink?" or when I hear a psychother-
apist say, "Drinking stems from underlying psychological problems," I know they didn't grow up in alcoholic families or they
are clinging to outmoded beliefs. This is not to say that alcoholism doesn't have a "cause" or is "unexplainable." It's to say that
widespread ignorance about the biology of alcohol addiction
is shocking. Virginia Yturaldi agrees. "When you have a habit,"
she told me, "you have a habit, an addiction—alcoholic—like any
other."

Alcoholics initially drink for the same reasons as everyone
else—to have a good time, to alter a mood, to lubricate a romance,
to brighten or shut out the workaday world, and on and on, until
addiction kicks in. Throughout my twenties just about everyone
drank heavily in the San Joaquin Valley. The culture allowed it.
It was a way of life, both on ranches and in towns. I did, too.
What I'm saying is everyone has enough reasons or excuses to
drink—lots of people have strained marriages, ranch life in the
San Joaquin Valley was tough on both men and women, though
many women with smarts and talent felt additionally smothered
under wifely expectations of the time—but not everyone reacts
to booze in an addictive way. Anyone who drinks enough can
become addicted. Others are predisposed to alcoholism with the
first drink. And yet the cause of the problem—a drug called alcohol—is something we avoided looking at for what it was.

When I quit drinking at thirty-two, it was only after I gained
a degree of understanding about how a child of alcoholics might
react to alcohol. My mother had alcoholic sisters, but we ignored
that clue. My father, seen as a long-suffering martyr to my mother's problem (until his own drinking became a problem), was
told the underlying cause of my mother's drinking and personality changes might be schizophrenia. Another popular belief
of the time was that drinking was a form of self-medication
for depression. Ignorance extended to my father's urging my

mother in a social situation to have just a "little drink," thereby protracting the drinking cycle and his participation as helpmate and martyr. We talked to a lot of people but all the wrong people. What we didn't understand was my mother didn't drink because she was crazy, she was crazy because she was drinking.

We didn't comprehend what was going on. Neither did others in those years. Like me, Donald Antrim felt that his father's martyrdom was honorable. "It seemed to me," he wrote, "that our family was guided by a bleak, incomprehensible fate. It wasn't incomprehensible, though, and it wasn't fate. It was alcohol." That statement isn't an oversimplification. To think of us in those years as creatures of free will is absurd. Free will for us didn't exist. With understanding and self-awareness can come some sort of personal freedom, but we didn't have it. As a result, our incomprehension did become fated. Ignorance drove us to live in servility to the commonplaces of our times. Just as limited horizons closed down our vision when winter fog rolled into the San Joaquin Valley, the same thing happened to our minds and spirits as the low, foggy horizon of possibility shut down around us, leaving us unable even to see a way out.

That's how I imagine my mother must've felt after she returned to the valley following a summer car trip to Nevada with my dad, my sister, and my sister's husband for a family wedding in Battle Mountain, my mother's birthplace, where her mother and some of her sisters and their families still lived. "We had such a good time," my sister Michele remembers. "Daddy and Mom were in such good moods." My mother stayed sober that weekend, laughed a lot, enjoyed the time with her mother, teased my brother-in-law about his long hippie hair, but on the drive back home to the valley, my sister recalls, she grew quieter and quieter. It was Sunday and my sister and her husband had to drive back to their home on the coast to go to work on Monday. My mother immediately retreated to her bed and lay with her back to the door when my sister came into the room to say good-bye. My mother didn't move when my sister spoke to her.

"We have to leave now," my sister said.

"Goodbye," my mother said.

I was back east, writing a dissertation for grad school, when four days later I got a call that my mother was dead. She'd gone on a binge, drinking gin, and must've felt herself suffocating because she flung herself out of bed onto the floor. That's how my father found her around 9:50 a.m. on August 3, 1972. He apparently put her back in bed before going outside to call my brother and say, "She's breathing her last." Mark was working for an ambulance company that summer and knew how to use two fingers to feel for a pulse under her jaw. She was already cold.

With understanding and self-awareness, as I've suggested, some sort of freedom might've arrived earlier, but I experienced release only after my mother had died and I returned from the funeral to my Cambridge apartment, where I resumed writing my dissertation. A few days later, after working at my desk for several hours, I lay on the couch and felt a great weight lift from my chest. I know this sounds made up, but it isn't. I sensed a surprising lightness around my heart. Only then did I grow aware of the pressing heaviness I'd carried in my chest, without my knowledge, for so many years.

Better now, I think, to end these memories closer to their beginning. I'm looking at some early photographs of my mother on horseback in California and Nevada. I have more photos than I realized of her on several different horses, some taken before I was born, and a playful thought causes me to wonder if part of her attraction to marrying a rancher was the opportunity to ride horses. In each photo she's smiling. In one she's about to gallop: the horse's hooves lift up, my mother's hair flies back. She looks happy and free.

CAPTURED!

THE SHERIFF OF WHITE PINE COUNTY, ELY, NEVADA, AN-
NOUNCES THE CAPTURE AT STEPTOE HOSPITAL,
ELY, NEVADA, ON FEB. 24, 1943, OF:

FRANK BERGON, JR., alias "BABYFACE", alias "TONY"

DESCRIPTION:

> AGE: Born February 24, 1943, at 8:35 a.m.
> PLACE OF BIRTH: Ely, Nevada
> HGT: 22 inches
> WGT: 7 lbs., 14 oz.
> HAIR: Brown (what there is of it)
> EYES: Shut
> COMPLEXION: Tomato Red
> BUILD: Mr. 5 x 5 Jr.
> OCCUPATION: Confidence man
> RELATIVES: Mr. and Mrs. Frank Bergon, Parents
>   695 Mill street, Ely, Nevada
>
> PECULIARITIES: Has sleepy appearance, looks like
>   midget, drinks Holstein cocktails,
>   wears jockey shorts, and speaks
>   with heavy accent—at times un-
>   intelligible.

All departments cancel wanted notice as subject placed on probation
to parents for life and restitution of stolen money made
good by his father, the poor guy.

Birth announcement for Frank "Tony" Bergon.

The FBI Rancher

When I was a boy, many of our dads and uncles grew more complicated in our eyes than simply "farmers" or "ranchers" because they'd been soldiers in the Second World War. Whether coming back from European foxholes or South Pacific warships or noncombat Alaskan depots, they returned from faraway lands as men with adventures their fathers never knew, shattering a stereotype of generational sameness on ranches and farms in the West. They distinguished themselves from their fathers and generated pride in their children. In this crowd of hallowed men with wartime auras, my dad stood out as singular for me and for others because for five years spanning the war he'd been a special agent for the FBI.

Those were years when the popular image of the FBI shined unsullied in the valley ranches and small towns, burnished by the derring-do of Hollywood's G-men toting submachine guns and TV's heroic undercover agent posing as a Communist in *I Led Three Lives*. America's safety, we believed, depended upon the FBI's vigilant pursuit of the gangsters, kidnappers, spies, and mobsters whose faces we studiously scrutinized on the wanted posters in the post office. We believed, too, in the bureau's web of social surveillance and its state-of-the-art scientific laboratories.

On a sunny morning, when walking across a vacant lot toward our elementary school, my friend Jim and I spotted some dried scat in the weeds that sparked our country-boy curiosity since we couldn't tell if it was animal or human.

"If we sent it to the FBI labs," I said, "they'd tell us."

Jim knowingly replied, "They'd tell us *who* it was from."

No wonder at the age of twelve, when I amateurishly typed a letter on my dad's clackety Remington manual typewriter to a pen pal named Gerald in Belgium, I identified myself as my father's son, Tony Bergon from Madera, California, U.S.A. "I might as well start from the beginning," I told Gerald. "I was born in Ely, Nevada. My father was a special agent for the Federal Bureau of Investigation (F. B. I.) and when I was born he had a bulletin printed resembling criminal captured posters, which he sent to his friends (like this one)." I included the birth announcement labeled "Captured" with my aliases listed as "Babyface" and "Tony."

My father was born Frank Alfred Bergon, but he later adopted the name of his dead brother and identified himself as Frank Albert Bergon. Because my dad and I didn't share middle names—mine was Anthony—I wasn't technically "Frank Jr." but always "Tony" until I went to elementary school, where the nuns wanted me to be "Francis," only to have my dad speed into town to straighten out that misnomer. Names are tricky things in relation to fathers and sons. I didn't want to be a junior, although some people do. I can only wonder how my father felt about his relationship to his father when, despite the stature bestowed on him as an FBI agent, he returned to the valley after the war with a wife and two children to be identified as the thirty-three-year-old son of a prominent rancher, his position freshly stenciled onto the door of the foreman's old black pickup: BERGON & SON RANCH CO.

Apparently destined for agricultural life, he'd been Madera High School's first president of the Future Farmers of America and the winner of California's statewide tree-judging championship, but he'd also been senior class president, student body vice president, high school newspaper editor, San Joaquin Valley champion debater, and the leading actor in the senior class play, *The Whole Town's Talking*. The high school newspaper, *The Maderan*, ran this front-page headline: SENIOR PLAY BIG HIT, AUDIENCE IS KEPT IN SPASMS.

20x30-inch postal card mailed from California to Washington, D.C., 1940.

"The fun centered around Frank Bergon," the article noted on Friday, June 7, 1929.

At the time he was only sixteen. He aspired to become a lawyer.

"What changed your mind?" I once overheard a relative ask.

"The Depression," my dad replied.

Three years after the Great Crash of October 1929, when he was nineteen, his mother died. She was thirty-nine. My father made a scrapbook honoring her memory with photos, drawings, a poem, and a final page picturing her grave. He worked as a night clerk in a hotel while studying accounting and business administration at a two-year commercial college in nearby Fresno, where he became a police officer and was picked to attend the National Police Academy in Washington, D.C., and Quantico, Virginia. Friends in the valley mailed him a twenty-by-thirty-inch, oversized, stiff-board "postal card," forty times normal size, requiring thirty-five two-cent stamps and five five-centers. The front of the card displayed a large pen-and-ink drawing of an old-time cop on a bicycle, his face a blow-up photo of my dad with an elaborate handlebar mustache sketched onto his upper lip and an old-style police helmet on his head.

Surrounding the figure on the bicycle, scattered every which way, were nearly a hundred notes and signatures from fellow cops and other Fresno friends, including the mayor, the chief of police, and the Grand Exalted Ruler of the Benevolent and Protective Order of Elks, most wishing him to hurry home. "The Dept. is going to pieces— come home," wrote attorney Dave "Big Hat" Peckinpah, father of the future film director Sam Peckinpah. Another well-wisher poeticized: "Tho you've gone from our gaze / Left the girls in a daze / We will bear up as Elks always do / But when you have returned / With that sheepskin hard earned / Won't the gang throw a party for you."

The affection embedded in these notes, hauled three thousand miles cross-country, I assume, by train and truck, responded to a genuine charm and empathy others found in my dad, including me. A big, pipe-smoking man with a thick head of hair and a hearty laugh, he could play any song you wanted to hear on one of his many harmonicas. While his importance shone on me, what made me feel more important was the personal closeness between us. As a small boy, I'd say "Let's wrestle, Daddy," and we'd lie on the living room floor with me stretched out on his chest and stomach until he'd roll me over to be on top without crushing me, then we'd roll again for me to be on top, and so on. That, to me, was wrestling. When I said "Show me your muscle," he pulled up his shirtsleeve and flexed. I was always astonished at how his bicep popped into the size of a grapefruit. Despite his strength, or maybe because of it, he never hit me, not once. Near-worship isn't too strong a description of how I felt about him. As a child I recall lying in bed feeling that I loved my dad so much I hoped I would die before he did.

I loved to ride around the ranch with him in his pickup. Sometimes while driving, with notes clipped to the truck visor, he would practice a speech he was going to give at one of his many organizations. He was an admired public speaker and storyteller, able to mix colloquial and formal diction in an intriguing, funny way. He could sing imitations of Al Jolson's songs exactly as they sounded on old 78 records. I don't remember him imitating Enrico Caruso, but he had a lot of his records, and books, too, surprising for a farmer, including a twenty-volume set of Dickens, a Conrad Argosy, *The Family Mark Twain*, Maupassant's short stories, a collected P. G. Wodehouse, Hemingway's *To Have and Have Not*, Melvin Purvis's *American Agent*, and the not-so-surprising collected poems of Edgar Guest.

As I grew older, we listened together to the fights on the radio, rooting for Jersey Joe Walcott against Rocky Marciano, because, as usual, even later during the era of TV's Friday Night Fights, we rooted for the underdog. We followed baseball together, and he taught me what to look for during the political conventions on TV. He was a Republican, but he admired Franklin Delano Roosevelt (recalling the sad moment when he pulled to the curb to listen to the report on the car radio of FDR's death). Although he voted for Ike, he rode through the valley on the train as a representative farmer with the Democratic presidential candidate, Adlai Stevenson, whose acuity and genuineness he praised when he came home. We didn't play sports together and didn't go on vacations, except once to Pismo Beach and once into the Sierras to visit our vacationing L.A. relatives, though he had to leave early to get back to the ranch. He didn't go on our scout camping trips with other men who took us, but every summer for five years he went around town to talk with parents to make sure that their kids, my friends, went to the weeklong Camp Chawanakee at Shaver Lake.

I was also happy to be the son of a father so much liked by my friends. A neighbor girl, who had conflicts with her own father, told me how she felt special and protected around my dad, who called her "kiddo," and told her "If you ever need any help, kid, you can always come to me." A high school buddy said that unlike his own remote doctor father my dad talked to us in a way that was in tune with what we were thinking. "He seemed to know what we were up to and could identify with us." When my school friend Bill visited the ranch one summer and was about to begin the long drive back to his Southern California home, my dad took him into town and bought four new tires for his car.

My father's need to check tire tread and air pressure before trips, an impulse familiar to all of us on the ranch, as well as to visiting relatives and friends, probably stemmed from his hurt back and a vague accident when he was a passenger and a car of agents flipped and one was killed. I say "vague" because I was a boy in the back seat of a car and overheard him telling this story, no doubt as a cautionary tale, to the driver next to him in the front seat, a friend speeding us down Highway 99. I never heard the story again because he didn't talk about his time in the FBI, at least not to me. My younger sister recalls only a brief anecdote. "He and some other G-men were on a train 'cause they were to keep an eye on a gangster who was also on the train. Daddy said he went and chatted the guy up and got in a poker game with him and his cronies while the other G-men sat back somewhere else. I have a feeling the FBI guys stood out like a sore thumb. Didn't they all tend to look alike?" When my sister later asked my father the gangster's name, he wouldn't tell her. "Either he figured I'd recognize the name," she said, "or maybe that he'd told me too much already." Agents in those years were taught to keep their mouths shut. Later revelations justly reviling the bureau and longtime director J. Edgar Hoover bothered my father, according to my aunt, for maligning the investigative integrity of agents he'd known, but he didn't defend or rationalize the director's despicable activity. He understandably said nothing to me during the sixties when my cynical view of much government activity extended to the bureau.

Routine investigative work, I suppose, would've been the bulk of what he did for the FBI, or mundane, somewhat scary tasks, like the assignment he mentioned of sitting up all night in a car in the Nevada sagebrush to guard a large Japanese fire balloon early in the war. Threats of attack at the time felt real. A Japanese submarine had surfaced in the Santa Barbara Channel and launched shells across the Pacific Coast Highway into oil storage tanks. Maybe because he was friends with the Mochizukis and had played music with them, one thing he mentioned is that the FBI didn't support Roosevelt's executive order that made possible the mass incarceration of people of Japanese ancestry in order to prevent espionage and sabotage.

His silence about criminals he encountered allowed my reading to take me deep into the violent mythology of Johnny Dillinger, Baby Face Nelson, and Pretty Boy Floyd. When my schoolteacher aunt saw me reading my father's copy of Melvin Purvis's *American Agent*, she asked, "Why don't you read about the saints?" At that age I was unable to explain how these criminals formed a mythical pantheon as richly exciting as any cosmic battle involving good and evil. To fashion a freshman high school report about the FBI and narcotics, I borrowed items stored in my father's den: an elaborate opium pipe (he sawed a notch in the stem to make it unusable before I could take it), used heroin needles, a jar of yen shee pellets, and his typed notes.

When I was in the seventh grade, we took into our house a boy whose father was an imprisoned gangster and mother an uncontrollable alcoholic (the boy's sisters went into other valley homes). For us it was an odd charitable gesture, given my mother's own alcoholism, but it reinforced a village myth of differences between respectable and derelict families. On our first night together in our shared bedroom, I asked my new eleven-year-old roommate what he wanted to be when he grew up. His flat-toned answer floated across the darkened room from where he lay in the other twin bed against the wall. "A criminal," he said. This response shocked my sense of the cosmos. Despite all my reading, gangsterism hadn't presented itself to me as a realistic career option. My new roommate, whose dad had worked for Bugsy Siegel–type gangsters, explained his visionary self-image. After a car chase, he told me, even one that might leave him crashed at the bottom of a San Francisco hill as it had his father, he would shoot it out with the pursuing FBI, not weakly give up like his cowardly father.

I asked my dad if he'd ever been in a shootout like those I'd been reading about, but his answer was brief and diverting:

something happened once from a distance with other agents behind a car, but he himself hadn't fired. We knew he could shoot because on the ranch when an irrigator pointed to an offending gopher quite far down a cotton row, a pest whose tunnels caused the loss of irrigation water, he pulled his .38 Special from his pickup glove compartment, gripped the pistol with both hands, aimed, and—with apparent indifference to the pressure of his foreman and several workers eyeing him—fired, knocking the gopher, as we discovered when it was retrieved, right through the eyes.

Years later, when I returned to Ely, Nevada, on a research trip to see the Mill Street apartment where I'd lived as a child, a retired deputy sheriff told me with utmost enthusiasm how much he'd learned about police work from my FBI father. "He taught me so much," he said. Like careful attention to all details, I suppose, even, for example, as my dad told me, when asking persons their names during an investigation and receiving a response as commonplace as Joe Smith, you still must ask, "How do you spell it?" After all, it might be spelled Smyth.

His objective investigative methods and his accounting skills can be seen in a hefty file folder he left behind labeled "Divorce Case," full of neatly written notes referring to his father as the defendant, or more accurately the "def," and his father's second wife, the plaintiff, as "pl." He mentioned to me in passing, and only once—never as a refrain signaling an excuse—how he returned to the ranch after the war because his father asked for his help. How much my grandfather's sticky divorce, ranch acquisitions in two counties, and partnerships with a half-dozen other ranchers hastened my father's return to ranching, I don't know. Some people think he would've stayed in the FBI or gone into other kinds of police work—he served on the local parole board and in retirement became a licensed private investigator—although contrary to these views, he once described to a reporter his nearly six years in the FBI as "an experience I wouldn't take a million dollars for, but an experience I wouldn't repeat for a million dollars, either."

What remains true is he never immersed himself in farming in the same way as my grandfather, loving the sweat and dirt of it, the heft of the shovel, the rattle of the tractor, the physicality of ranch animals. He did the figures and managed a business. His heart was elsewhere. He threw himself into civic life as a member of many town organizations and valley farm associations. He genuinely loved the San Joaquin Valley and his hometown, Madera, in the center of the state, as the best place to live in the world. Honors like "Citizen of the Year" came his way as well as statewide positions in the California Farm Bureau and the Council of California Growers. When he was elected president of the Western Cotton Growers Association, valley newspaper editorials touted him as the best man to become Governor Reagan's next secretary of agriculture.

The California State Senate issued a resolution honoring him for his community and agricultural leadership. A colorfully lettered, gilt-edged, embossed copy of Senate Resolution No. 114, listing his many awards and activities, now hangs in the upstairs hallway of my house. Recently a workman, who was refinishing the wooden floors beneath the citation, told me he'd read the account of my dad on the wall. "They don't make them like that anymore," he said.

The senate resolution didn't mention the FBI. Neither did it mention the disarray our home life had become, manifested in my mother's drinking. Nor did it mention the number of times he'd been operated on for bleeding ulcers until removal of three-quarters of his stomach stanched that periodic problem. He could still tell stories, cook omelets and soups, produce laughter, juggle several community projects with high energy, and rapidly type long, frequent single-spaced letters to us kids at boarding schools and colleges, but an air of tension and disappointment enveloped him, increasingly so after his father's death ("Frank wasn't the same after your grandfather died," a friend told me) and my mother's death ("Your dad was never the same after Lina's death," a cousin maintained). Booze took over his life.

"Your dad missed his calling," a longtime friend on a neighboring ranch told me.

"What was his calling?" I asked.

"I don't know," my friend replied, "but he missed it."

While growing up I don't recall any pressure to do or be anything in particular, nor do I remember money ever talked about in my family as a particularly valuable thing in itself to strive for. My father's claimed unwillingness to take a million dollars for his FBI experience was more than a platitude. What we learned was Depression-era frugality. To this day, Holly, my wife, jokingly calls me "the French Peasant." The money we got we earned, beginning for me at six years old with a quarter a week for chores, rising to a quarter an hour for chopping cotton when I was twelve. After filling out time sheets, I deposited my pay into my first savings account in the Crocker-Anglo National Bank. A visiting friend of my parents at the time, a school superintendent, saw me coming in from work at sundown one Saturday evening after weeding cotton for ten hours, and asked, "Doesn't your father know there are child labor laws?"

My practical eighth-grade teacher and head of the convent, Sister Charles, took me aside one day and said my family was economically ideal for a happy life: we didn't have a lot of money, she said, but we didn't have too little, either. In contrast to much California agribusiness, my father was self-described in a

Western Cotton Growers journal as an "average farmer." Land rich, cash poor was the cliché I heard more than once.

While I felt it was up to me to decide what I wanted to do or be, it was, in his view, not going to be on the ranch. Citing the increasingly tough economics of making a living in agriculture, my father wrote a booklet titled "Why My Sons Aren't Going to Farm." My brother later joked that the title should've been "My Sons Aren't Going to Farm Because I'm Going to Sell the Ranch." We were always told, no matter what happened to the bulk of the ranch, the original forty-acre "home place," where my grandfather in 1920 began farming grapes and cotton, would stay in the family. It didn't turn out that way. Booze hastened bad decisions and the loss of Depression-era virtues. The ranch, already shrunken from piecemeal sales, vanished in a final desperate sale. The ranch went under and the money it generated quickly dissipated, following the trajectory of a classic American immigrant-family story in three generations: The first generation gets a foothold in the new land, the second makes a fortune, and the third blows it. Now the story extends to the fourth generation, who writes about it.

None of these ranch losses generated much conversation with my two sisters, my brother, or me. We didn't discuss the disappointment we felt. Like many children of alcoholics, we didn't talk about a lot of things. Aside from my brother's joking remark, only one other mention about the final ranch sale comes to mind, a passing comment from one of my sisters, less complaining than wistful: "I think we should've been consulted." What did concern us was our father's sixteen years of drunkenness and our failed interventions until his death from a stroke at age seventy-four. Because I was older and away, back east at school for the most part, during those years of my father's decline, his alcoholism didn't overwhelm me as had my mother's when I was a child, though it became revelatory. I came to see how his stance as the long-suffering husband of a drunken wife depended on ways he helped support her drinking while disguising his own growing alcoholism. The bitterness I felt toward him in his drunkenness totally altered me from the little boy I once was, when affection for my dad had caused me to lie in bed hoping I'd die before he did. Estrangement replaced affection.

Now here comes the mystery of life after death, what's remembered and what's forgiven. Death shakes away the flaws not essential to our character and illuminates the things that are. When my father died, despite the sixteen years of drinking that strained other relationships besides mine, the church was packed. I gave the eulogy and spoke with affection of how he taught us the necessity of countering life's obvious unfairness with our own constant efforts to be fair. A former worker walked in his cowboy boots down the church aisle after viewing my dad in his casket and told me, "He was the best man I ever worked for." One of the few local organizations my father didn't direct or lead, serving only as a working member, the St. Vincent de Paul Society, was also, I think, his favorite. As a boy, I rode with him in the pickup as he hauled groceries to people in country shacks. I heard his former foreman Sonny recall the same thing. "We loaded up the truck several times in one day," he told me when I returned years after my father's death to do some research for a valley novel. "He helped a lot of people in this valley," a friend told me. A county supervisor recalls how after giving his first nervous speech as a young man in the Toastmasters' Club, he received a typed letter from my dad complimenting him on the good job he'd done. "It meant a lot to me," he said. "I still have the letter."

A new senior center was named after him. He used to go to an earlier one to play his harmonica and get the older folks singing and tapping their toes.

Despite revelations of the malfeasance of the FBI and his beloved J. Edgar, which increasingly pained him, the aura of his bureau connection, complicating his farmer image, continued to give him stature in the eyes of many valley residents. While interviewing people for my novel, I introduced myself over the phone to one man I didn't know by mentioning my father. Immediately over the line came a jubilant shout, "FBI!"

After my first novel was published, I was giving a radio talk-show interview in Winnemucca, Nevada. The first call from a listener was from a man who said he'd heard me on his car radio and pulled off to find a pay phone. "Hey," he said, "I knew your dad."

My brother, Mark, reminded me how our dad went off on a rant after a neighbor had justified some financial mistreatment of another neighbor by saying "Business is business." Our dad mockingly repeated the cliché to puncture the notion of business as an amoral enterprise justifying the absence of compassion. On the ranch, he would go into the backyard, where he'd moved the cabin of Old Man Lascurain, the farmworker my grandfather had hired in the 1920s, and rub the old man's feet during the last year of his life to make him feel better, embodying the eighteenth-century adage that the true measure of people is revealed in how they treat someone who can do them absolutely no good.

My life's accumulation of memories and feelings about my father had become so complicated I thought I'd never be able to sort them out enough to write an essay like this one about him. My disappointment and estrangement had grown too strong. I wanted to hide my embarrassment. What freed me was writing a novel with a character who wasn't him but was like him in many ways. After the fact I realized what I really thought and felt about him. Without my consciously attempting to write about my father, what emerged in fiction was the portrait of a man with a good heart, unliberated from the paternalistic and chauvinistic code of his upbringing. The clarification of my emotional turmoil was revelatory: what I felt for this man who was like my father was love.

When this novel, set in the San Joaquin Valley, was completed, the local historian and columnist Bill Coate interviewed me for the town newspaper. It turned out he wanted to talk at length about my thoughts on why my father was so loved in the area. He told me how my dad had helped him when he was doing historical research about an old-time judge. I mentioned that my dad owned the book *Will Rogers: The Story of His Life* and believed in the possibility of Rogers's claim that he'd never met a man he didn't like. My interviewer probed for something deeper. I talked about possibilities connected to certain memories of his good-humored storytelling and paternal kindnesses, an ability to show he cared. Bill Coate agreed, adding, "He made me feel important."

When the newspaper article appeared in *The Madera Tribune* about my return to the valley to give a reading from my new novel, *Jesse's Ghost*, it carried an earlier photo of me next to my father with his hand on my shoulder, under the ambiguous headline, "Frank Bergon Returns Home." On a subsequent visit during a high school reunion, when I was to give a talk about the "true story" behind my valley novel, I arrived at the Madera building on South D Street named the Frank Bergon Senior Center. A long-forgotten sense of pride and identity returned along with laughter when a neighbor from my youthful ranch days offered me this reminder with her own wry smile, as she aptly told me, "In this town, you are Frank Bergon's son."

Magic in Cowboy Country

The most amazing magic trick I saw as a kid took place in my family's ranch house when I was ten years old. After doing my pedestrian late-afternoon chores of burning the trash, dumping the garbage, and feeding the chickens, I walked into the house through the kitchen and was about to cross the threshold into the living room when I saw my father in his ranch clothes, outlined in bronze sunlight against the west-facing windows.

He called me by the nickname only he used, "Stay there, Buck. Look at this."

I stood in the doorway between rooms. My father dangled from his fingers a tricolored silk scarf, resembling a cobra with a green body, flared white hood, and wedge-shaped scarlet head. The exoticism of the colored foulard in contrast to the ordinariness of everything around it, including my father, stunned me.

Holding the snakelike silk by its corner tail, he reached down with his free hand, grabbed the triangular head, and tied the silk into a knot. Slowly the red head, pointing toward the floor, curled upward and moved by its own power through the knot, untying itself. A dizzying sensation engulfed me. I felt myself floating free from the everyday ranch and the earth itself. For the first time I'd seen real magic. My way of seeing the world never again would be the same.

My dad handed me the silk and showed me how to do the trick. He also gave me two beautifully constructed boxes, one of mahogany, the other of teak, for making cards and coins vanish.

He'd apparently dabbled in magic when he was young. That he could do something extraordinary in an ordinary ranch house wasn't surprising. One day he pulled out of the closet an old violin and played what I hear in memory as a riff from a concerto. I never heard him play again and the violin disappeared. Only in 2016, nearly thirty years after his death, did I discover that on senior class day during his high school graduation he was part of a trio. Two fellow students on the piano and clarinet joined him on the violin, playing "Beside the Western Sea," labeled "very good" in the school newspaper.

On the wall of his book-lined den hung framed charcoal sketches he'd drawn. The most haunting showed ducks flying through a mysterious chiaroscuro of clouds. I found in a file several cartoons with an instructor's commentary from a brief correspondence course he took with the Raye Burns School of Cartooning in Cleveland for ten dollars a month. I never learned anything about him as a magician or where he bought such well-made tricks. Death closed the door on that information.

What prompted his afternoon performance and gifts was my burgeoning interest in magic, which skyrocketed after I saw the movie *Houdini*, starring Tony Curtis and Janet Leigh. I came home from the library with books on the history of magic and how-to books. I read everything I could about Houdini, who became my secular saint. I studied photos of him. In the age of bulked-up bodybuilders like Joe Weider and Charles Atlas, I wanted a more naturally strong body like Houdini's as seen in photos of him stripped and bent over in chains and padlocks. His daring, risky escapes extended magic beyond entertainment to a matter of life and death. I wanted to be a professional magician.

Magic and reading became my solo entertainments. As a ranch boy, I spent much time alone. The older of my two sisters had friends her age on a vineyard two miles away, but no boys my age lived that close. After school and on weekends, I was pretty much on my own. Even at work driving a tractor or irrigating I was mostly by myself. I had plenty of time to live in my imagination.

I began with a magic kit before receiving my father's pre-war boxes and silk. I learned from books how to do tricks with everyday things like napkins, eggs, and matches. I juggled plates and threw knives. From five volumes of *Tarbell's Course in Magic* I practiced sleight-of-hand with cards and coins. I discovered magic companies whose mail-order tricks could be somewhat trusted to match their elaborate catalog descriptions. I subscribed to *Genii: The Conjurors' Magazine* and began to do shows, mostly for kids in their homes, and then on the stage of the parish hall, where my younger sister opened the performance with her Japanese parasol dance.

The town's sole amateur magician performed the first live shows I attended. Ed Hirsch, a soft-spoken insurance salesman and the plainest of men, became a wizard when he flipped through a children's black-and-white coloring book that became instantly technicolored. I wanted something more. At home I was designing my escape from a crate into which I would be tied and nailed and thrown into the Madera Irrigation District Canal. My failure to figure out how to make the wooden box sink was, I suppose, fortunate.

At the Madera County Fair I saw my first professional magician, who duplicated Houdini's "Metamorphosis," the illusion where the prestidigitator switches places with a pretty assistant tied into a large bag and placed in a steamer trunk. It was an ordinary trick, though I did attend more than one performance. Afterward I followed the magician around to get a chance to talk to him. Offstage, he was an ordinary young guy with pomaded hair combed straight back, even a bit shabby in his worn black suit. When we entered the men's restroom together at the fairgrounds, he turned to a fellow carnival itinerant and said, "This is my fan," which reduced me in a way I didn't want to be reduced because I saw myself soon living on the road with the carnival as he was.

More intriguing to me at the county fair were the sideshow performers. Houdini wrote about fire-eaters and snake handlers as fellow artists. One autumn night, in a dimly lit tent, while a violent, crop-destroying rain pounded the canvas, a man ate fire and pierced his cheek with a nail. He then held up a thin foot-long spike, something like a shiny kebab skewer. He rolled up his shirtsleeve and asked a kid standing next to me to grip his bicep and tricep, separating them. The sideshow performer, another ordinary-looking guy who could've just come in from working in the fields, aimed the sharp metal point at the kid's throat with the warning, "Don't let go." He jammed the spike through his arm. "Now you can let go." After we had a chance to register what we were seeing, he slowly pulled out the penetrating steel. Blood trickled down his arm. This was no illusion. The spike had gone through his arm.

When I later passed the tent, the night rain had stopped and the arm-piercer had transformed into a carney with a microphone enticing fairgoers to come inside and see the show's freaks and wonders. His white shirt displayed a bloodstained sleeve.

Like Houdini, I loved all the oddities of the everyday world, people and events that bent the normal. Houdini maintained a friendship with an armless violin player (she played with her toes). I devoured paperbacks of *Ripley's Believe It or Not*. I made a scrapbook with stenciled letters on the cover, TAKE IT OR LEAVE IT, and pages of magazine- and newspaper-clipped photos and stories about a two-headed baby (featured in *Life*), a tightrope-walking fox, a Colorado man able to read eight thousand words a minute, the world's first parachutist (a woman), the world's oldest Bible (1,500 years old in the Library of Congress), a man stabbed in a Miami bar who didn't feel the knife sticking out of his back (the blade had passed through his spinal column without harm), a Grand Coulee waterfall reversed by wind and flying straight into the sky—all real-world wonders bordering on the magical because they shocked usual expectations, or what I'd been led to believe was the normal world. That's why I loved magic performed outside on a rough stage at the county fair or my own shows in the scruffy parish hall rather than on TV or in a fancy theater. Magicians or sideshow carnies who revealed wonders under a cloudy valley sky amid the smells of vineyards and wet pastures were those I wanted to emulate.

The oddities of history also fascinated me. Even my ordinary hometown of Madera offered something extraordinary in world history. I taped into my scrapbook two wooden scraps, labeled like religious relics "Wood from the Flume," next to a newspaper-syndicated "Strange but True" account and sketch of the "Longest Boardwalk in the World," paralleling the logging flume that once "extended 63 miles…from the Sierra Nevadas… to Madera, Cal." The underlining was mine.

When I was thirteen I met Thomas Dethlefsen, owner of the Golden Gate Magic Company on Market Street in San Francisco. An inventor who demonstrated new tricks on his shop's stage, Tom, as everyone called him, was an older gentleman with a welcoming smile, known for encouraging young magicians. With tufts of white hair on both sides of his bald head, he reminded me of the famous Harry Blackstone, who'd received the mantel of magic from the illusionist Howard Thurston, who in a business deal inherited the wand from the father of modern American magic, Harry Keller, who in turn called Houdini "The Greatest." I knew all about magicians and their performances—the startling coin magic of T. Nelson Downs, the fabulous card sleights of Dai Vernon, the bullet-catching act of the "Queen of Magic" Adelaide Herrman, and the failed, fatal bullet-catching performance of Chung Ling Soo—because I'd read about them and seen them all in the solitude of my imagination, a stage for magical wonders I never came close to witnessing in reality.

The magicians I liked best were skeptical dreamers who created magical worlds they didn't believe in. Believe what you see, I was told in the hardheaded world. My magicians, the most rational of humans, admonished the opposite: Don't always believe what you see but believe what illusions point to: the inexplicable world as it is. A spinning silk transformed into a cane that then sprouts roses out of which appear wing-flapping doves reveals the primacy of nature's metamorphoses, a primal way of seeing the transmogrifying powers of the cosmos that I didn't understand, couldn't understand, and would never understand.

Tom Dethlefsen encouraged me to go on to high school but to forget about college and to start performing. College wouldn't help me become a magician. He liked the way I structured my act, the sequence and rhythm of my routine, its tension and drama, but I already felt my professional ambition lapsing into recognition that I wasn't good enough.

When I was fourteen, I received a letter from Tom, saying, "Glad to know you are putting on shows with Ed Hirsch. Keep it up. It's lots of fun."

Lots of fun, to be sure, but also much more, even for Tom, who I later learned was a founding member of the Fellowship of Christian Magicians, dedicated to spreading the Gospel. Members signed a statement of faith in the equally important tenets of biblical infallibility, virgin birth, resurrection, bodily ascension, and a code of ethics forbidding exposure of magical effects and ideas.

I'd shared the magic of religion as an altar boy when taught to believe that the world of appearance isn't the real world. With Thomistic concepts of form and matter, I could define the transubstantiation of wafers and wine into divinity's real presence at daily mass. I could differentiate between the virgin birth and the

Immaculate Conception. A greater reality engulfing our illusory life, I was taught, offered the comforting though perilous solution of life after death.

My fascination with magic began moving me away from religious miracles I never saw while revealing the often unnoticed mystery of the world around me. Like reading, magic was more than entertainment in the way it took me out of myself. It shocked my senses and elevated my perception. It shattered certitudes. The earth seemed to disappear from under me—the everyday earth I took for granted—when watching the inanimate silk in my father's hands come alive as a snake moving under its own power. A similar out-of-the-ordinary shock happened earlier when I was very young and I saw my father and grandfather walk into the ranch yard covered with blood, their pants and shirts soaked red. My dad, seeing my disturbance and fear, quickly told me they'd been dehorning cattle, something I would see as a more ordinary ranch occurrence when I was older and watched blood spurt from the heads of dehorned cattle. My dad and grandfather weren't hurt, as I'd thought. I'd been shocked by an illusion.

Illusion attached to danger and pain, as Houdini knew, opened doors to the sublime, something I must have sensed when designing the wooden crate into which I planned to be tied, nailed, and tossed into a canal. The "idea" of bodily pain and danger, Edmund Burke wrote in his essay on the "Sublime and Beautiful," in all "modes and degrees of labour, pain, torment, is productive of the sublime; and nothing else in this sense can produce it." I began to see how magical illusions could move me from the real torments of my life to what was beautiful and sublime without shackling me to illusions of the supernatural.

Magic as a literal transaction with the supernatural is something Houdini vehemently denied. "Ladies and Gentlemen," he announced onstage in a vatic voice, still startling in its intensity today on YouTube, as he introduced what he called "my original invention, the Water Torture Cell, although there is nothing supernatural about it."

Many, though, did believe Houdini possessed superhuman powers to escape when they saw him hanging upside down, cramped, and padlocked, unable to breathe in the water-filled, glass-fronted water torture cell. His biographer Kenneth Silverman, in *Houdini!!! The Career of Ehrich Weiss*, reports how Arthur Conan Doyle believed Houdini's "dematerializing and reconstructing force" allowed his escapes from handcuffs. "My reason tells me that you have this wonderful power," Doyle told Houdini, "for there is no alternative." Doyle could invent the world's most superrational detective but deny Houdini's explanation of a simple spiritualist's trick. "It could only have been done by dematerialization," Doyle insisted, "no other way."

I saw how Doyle was not alone in a need to believe the uncanny. Others insisted how Houdini's ability to dematerialize himself also explained his ability to pass in a few seconds through a brick-and-mortar wall that an audience had watched Bricklayers Union No. 34 build on a Boston stage. Three-sided screens were placed on each side of the wall, with Houdini in one. According to *The Boston Globe*, Houdini's hands waved above the screen. "Here I am," he cried. "Now I'm gone." Immediate removal of the screens, according to the newspaper, revealed Houdini on the opposite side of the wall, "smiling serenely at the mystification of the clever ones."

I admired magicians because they didn't believe in magic. They always knew there was a trick. I was stunned to learn how some psychics and spiritualists claimed Houdini himself was a powerful medium even as he exposed their ways. In his twenties as a tent-show and curio hall magician, he'd quit doing tricks that apparently produced spirit communications because, as he said, "I most certainly did not relish the idea of treading on the sacred feelings of my admirers." But when Spiritualism as a religion filled a moral vacuum for many in response to the battlefield slaughters of the First World War, Houdini waged a crusade against flimflammers hoodwinking the gullible.

The gullible, I came to see, included most of humanity. While crossing the Atlantic by steamship, Houdini performed a spiritualist's trick for his fellow passengers, including former president Theodore Roosevelt, who'd written in secret on a scrap of paper, "Where was I last Christmas?" Before the paper was unfolded to reveal the question, Houdini uncovered a previously blank slate to show the site of Roosevelt's holiday travels in a chalked map of South America.

Next morning on deck, Roosevelt put his arm around Houdini and asked him "man to man" if he'd acquired the map through genuine spiritualism. "No, Colonel," Houdini responded, "it was hocus pocus."

Most people, then as now, believe in some form of magic as a way of giving the cosmos meaning and of controlling occult powers they want to believe exist. The stage actress Sarah Bernhardt asked Houdini if he could restore her amputated leg. It became increasingly apparent to me through my reading that thousands of people came to see him risk his life in order to help them feel triumphant, if only momentarily, over the danger and fear they spent a lot of their time trying to manage, mostly through magical means, especially the appalling prospect of their own absolute personal death in an oblivious cosmos.

In his campaign against death and nothingness, Houdini in chains and handcuffs almost broke his neck diving headfirst into the ocean off an Atlantic City pier. In a San Francisco park, manacled to a burning stake, he managed to escape after the wind shifted and ignited his clothes. In Fort Worth, he escaped with his hands tied behind his back while a motorcycle dragged him down Main Street. Buried alive in Los Angeles, he nearly lost consciousness clawing his way up through the dirt. "The audience never knows whether the stunt is easy or hard," he said.

When defining himself, Houdini avoided the term "magician." Testifying against fraudulent psychics before a congressional committee, he replied when asked his occupation, "I am a mystifier, which means I am an illusionist.... I am human.... But I do tricks nobody can explain." Even when explanations were visible, as when he twisted and contorted to escape from a straitjacket while hanging upside down from a skyscraper a hundred feet above gawkers in the street, he remained a mystifier, not as to how he was escaping, but why. "Like great unsolved crimes," Silverman writes, "his escapes offend the wish to live without ambiguity. They itch for solution." Houdini didn't offer solutions. He refuted solutions to mystery like those of Spiritualism. In the ambiguous world of magic, great magicians, lacking faith in magic and magical thinking, question our certitudes. "I am sincere in my endeavor for the truth," Houdini wrote, but he didn't proclaim a final truth. He was always on the edge of telling us we live in a universe without the meaning we might ascribe to it.

After entering high school, I put away the things of magic at the same time I discovered the power of language to create illusions. That discovery offered an ecstatic flash. Writing and reading in solitude allowed magical elevations of perception. Words could conjure up a scene of a Béarnais American rancher in a work hat, Levi's, and rolled-up sleeves, his wrinkled brow and tired sweaty face rapt in the late-afternoon autumnal light coming through the windowpanes from across the pasture and the cattle behind him. From his fingers dangled a snakelike silk mysteriously slithering free from a knot. It was both ordinary and magical to experience through words how it felt and what it meant to be alive in such a moment.

At an end-of-the-summer ranch barbecue before my return to college for the fall semester, I retrieved from a closet the black, gold-beaded magician's table I'd bought from Tom Dethlefsen, a silk top hat once worn by a family friend in a fraternal organization, and a few old magic tricks to entertain the cowboys and fieldworkers at the ranch party in our screened-in patio. I had every intention of then putting the paraphernalia away forever, but one of the cowboys, Darrell Winfield, asked me when I returned home for the Christmas holidays to do a show for his five kids. And I did.

The Winfields lived in a ranch house on the San Joaquin River. Darrell's children sat on the floor in front of the Christmas tree, five blond specks of consciousness as I ate razor blades and made milk disappear from a newspaper cone I then tossed into the air to become a red bouquet of silk flowers. I fanned repeatedly shrinking cards until they vanished, caused rice to multiply and turn into water, restored to wholeness a cut rope and a torn napkin, made coins, silks, and lighted cigarettes disappear and reappear, and so forth, all tricks with more impact than skill, magical effects I liked that seemed to border on danger (swallowing razor blades), vulnerability (letting milk leak from the newspaper), and exposure (pretending to reveal a trick without doing so)—all ordinary stuff edging toward the extraordinary.

Perhaps afterward, as magic sometimes achieved for me, the children would marvel at the sheer existence of milk, flowers, and even razor blades.

Like my dad, Darrell Winfield had an influence on my career as a magician because I would've again put away the tricks except that Darrell, acting as my fan and unofficial agent, arranged some shows in valley bars during the next summer. I became a magician in cowboy country. Cowboys make good magic fans because they love playing tricks on each other. For the drinking crowd, I added a bit of the risqué. A pink bra popping into the air from a cowgirl's cleavage produced hoots and hollers.

On the patio of a cowboy bar in town, where Darrell had arranged another show, I announced that I would perform the world's greatest card trick. I would dematerialize three chosen cards in a deck that someone in the crowd held in a sealed envelope and pass them invisibly into another sealed envelope held by someone else on the other side of the room. A cowboy shouted, "A hundred dollars says he can't." The greedy, I'd come to learn, are easiest to fool. Darrell replied, "A hundred dollars says he can." While the show was stopped for a third cowboy to collect and hold the money, Darrell told the bartender to give me another drink. "The more he drinks," Darrell said, "the better he is." It wasn't true, but the trick worked, and Darrell won the bet, although he didn't care whether he would win or lose. That's only money. A true cowboy cares about nothing more than being a cowboy.

That was probably the last show I did, except one more for Darrell's children in another of their valley ranch houses. Several years later, when my wife, Holly, and I visited the Winfields after they'd moved to a Wyoming horse ranch, I gathered together a couple of tricks because I'd heard that twelve-year-old Brian Winfield was doing magic. "How did you eat the razor blades?" Brian asked when we arrived on the ranch. "He'll never tell you," his sister Nancy said. I gave Brian a gaff for vanishing lighted cigarettes and a couple of other tricks. In the eighth grade, he placed a classmate in a cardboard box and sawed him in half.

At that time Darrell had been discovered in Wyoming by the Leo Burnett advertising agency and was in his seventh year as the main Marlboro Man. I thought it was stupendous that every ranch kid on horseback in the West aspired to be the Marlboro Man, while his son wanted to be a magician.

Forty years later, because of my lifelong friendship with Darrell, I was asked to give the eulogy at his memorial service. As people gathered at his family ranch, I overheard his daughter Nancy talking to Holly. "He would never tell me how he did his tricks." She was talking about me. "I had such a crush on him," she told Holly. "He was nineteen, and I thought he was so handsome." She wiggled her fingers in the air like dancing flames. "And he did magic!"

Why do revelations of magic's side benefits come so late?

After my eulogy, I heard a horse whinny outside the enormous horse barn, where the ceremony took place. Darrell's grandson led the riderless horse into the eerily silent barn, and his son, Brian, removed the saddle with Darrell's boots hanging upside down from the stirrups. Outside, the horse was freed into the pasture. Darrell's daughter Debi later sent me a pair of his heart-stamped spurs.

At the memorial service, I sat on a hay bale in the big horse barn and listened to an Arapaho singer beat a drum and chant for his dead friend. I'd visited Darrell just four months before he died. He was there on the ranch. Then he was gone.

Since I'd first met him, I'd published four novels and dedicated one to him. I'd written a magazine article about magic as an art of deception. All my novels, as I'd come to realize, shared the same theme: the tragedy and necessity of human self-deception.

At the memorial, I recalled going into a hospital for a procedure and trying to stay alert for the moment I passed from consciousness. I wanted to remember the last breath I took as I entered the darkness. It didn't happen. I had no memory of a transition. I woke as I was being wheeled out of surgery. I was there. Then I wasn't. I'd vanished but came back. That was a pretty good trick. But I intimated another. You're there. Then you're not. Forever. That's the best trick of all.

My L.A. Relatives

Horses on our San Joaquin Valley ranch when I was a boy served as tools for rounding up cattle—not for recreation—so the few times I climbed into the saddle just for fun happened when our relatives from Los Angeles showed up and wanted to go horseback riding. That's when the gap between city and ranch folks loomed as wide as a country mile.

My cousins were warned, "Don't turn their heads toward the barn." The horses would then think it was time to go home, because when we finished cutting, branding, and doctoring cattle we usually raced from the corrals down the dirt road to the barn.

No way could my two young cousins or their father, Cousin Eddie, slow the horses one morning after they neglected the warning and found themselves on a wild ride back to the barn, lucky to cling to the saddles and to duck their heads fast enough to avoid getting whacked as the runaway horses rushed through the barn door and finally stopped at the feed trough, waiting to get unsaddled.

With the day's ride abruptly ended—the horses refused to be coaxed from the barn—Cousin Eddie unbuckled the saddle from the big roan named Red but incorrectly jerked the reins over its ears. Red reared up on his hind legs, worrying me that its front hooves might crush my cousin's skull. Cousin Eddie responded to this close call with a happy smile. I remember thinking at the time, *Don't these city people know how to do anything?* Shining in the barn that day was how city and country people live in different worlds, and they always have, in the way they see, think, and feel. Not necessarily better or worse, I came to realize. They were still Californians, but different. My L.A. relatives helped define who I was and wasn't.

Cousin Eddie

Cousin Eddie considered himself lucky. He remarked on his luckiness even when he was young, just turned twenty-one, after getting some money from Uncle Lawrence and driving with friends for a little fun at the Cal-Neva casinos. "We pulled the car off the road to sleep," he told me, "and flipped coins to see who got the back seat. I did. I was lucky that way. The other guys had to sleep in the front seat or out on the ground." With his boyish good looks, athletic build, and intense brown eyes, Cousin Eddie had the friendly manner I associated with movie stars in L.A. His sense of his own good luck led me to wonder whether he inherited his joie de vivre and engaging smile from his Béarnais American mother, who was my grandfather's oldest sister, someone I never knew, or from his spindly, joking German American father, Uncle Oscar, who wore suspenders and entertained us kids with his funny monologues in mock Russian or Chinese.

Handsome, charming Cousin Eddie in his neatly pressed army uniform comes across in old photos as a radiant G.I. Joe. "I was drafted in November 1941," he said, "and after boot camp in St. Louis, Missouri, I got into the Army Air Corps, in charge of equipment and supplies. From Tacoma we took the train up to Fairbanks, Alaska, and we were all set to be shipped to Africa with desert equipment, but Dutch Harbor got bombed and we didn't have to go. We were lucky."

On a leave, during the war, he traveled by bus to visit my folks in Ely after I was born. It was night as the bus approached town after hours of desolate stretches on Route 50, later dubbed by *Life* magazine "the Loneliest Road in America." Eddie was dozing when the bus pulled off the road and stopped in response to the blinking lights of a state trooper's car behind it. The driver opened the door, and from the back of the bus Eddie heard an official voice announce, "FBI. Is Sergeant Peschke aboard this bus?" Eddie grabbed his duffel from the luggage rack and climbed down the steps to meet my dad, who joined him in the back seat of the trooper's car. "We drove into Ely with the lights still flashing," Cousin Eddie later told me, a thrilling ride after the long bus trip. "First class all the way."

After the war, Eddie married the woman we knew as Cousin Mary, a lovely valley girl from Selma he'd met when she was working for the phone company in Taft, where she'd moved with her first husband, who was stationed at Gardner Army Airfield. "He was a fighter pilot," Cousin Eddie explained about Mary's first husband. "You know how they are, sleeping with any gal coming your way, because there's only today and no tomorrow." Fighter pilots faced danger even in the San Joaquin Valley. Thirty-seven cadets and officers died in training flights at the Taft airfield during the war. Mary's husband survived but their marriage didn't. "They'd been married a year or less when they divorced," Cousin Eddie said. "It was a tough life in Taft."

Besides their summer visits to the ranch, when we loaded up their car with lugs of grapes and apricots for the trip back to L.A., we once visited Cousin Eddie and Cousin Mary at Dinkey Creek, in the mountains above Madera, where they vacationed with their two boys. An urban salesman all his life and eventually manager of the Baker Oil Tools Company, Cousin Eddie had the leisure of regular vacations, something my dad didn't know as a rancher. The one time my father joined us at Dinkey Creek, the visit was brief; he had to get back down to the valley after a day or two, leaving us with our cousins. We thought Cousin Mary quite fetching, sunning herself in a two-piece suit on top of a granite boulder, amid the roaring stream of Dinkey Creek, which was named not for its size but for someone's dog. I now know Cousin Eddie, swimming nearby and enjoying his vacation, felt himself lucky to have avoided a farmer's plight.

At ninety, still nimble and boyish in khaki shorts, Cousin Eddie ended up in an assisted-living apartment at a senior care home in Visalia, a valley town under a sky thick with polluting dust from dairy farms. An urbanite all his life, he now lived in the San Joaquin Valley near his country relatives, who farmed in a way he never wanted to do. Though a bit miffed at no longer being allowed to drive, he made a joke of it. He was an active officer of the senior care board, and the engagement calendar above his neatly arranged desk showed squares marked with several events.

When I reminded him of the horse's hooves missing his head long ago on the ranch, he smiled with the same cheerfulness he showed that day in the barn despite the disrupted ride. "I've always been a lucky guy," he told me.

Still irrepressibly cheerful at ninety, he reflected on his luckiness. When the war started and before he'd met Mary, he had another girlfriend in L.A., a beautiful Cal graduate with a rich father, a manager of Bank of America, who owned many Southern California lemon and orange groves. "She asked me to marry her," Cousin Eddie said, "but I didn't want to leave her alone—this was in '41—while I was in the army. I told her to marry another friend of hers, named Bogie, who was also rich and a Cal grad like her. It was a better fit. We all got together after the war."

I wondered how this turn of events squared with Cousin Eddie's vision of himself as a lucky guy. "You could've married a gorgeous rich woman," I said. "You gave up the chance for lots of money and an easy life. How does that make you lucky?"

Cousin Eddie cocked his head at me curiously, as though to say *I know a few things you don't*. "Maybe so," he said, "but then I would've ended up a sour lemon farmer, working for her dad."

Cousin André

Many of my L.A. relatives stay in my mind as indoor people, like my Uncle John Costahaude, my grandmother's brother, whose asthma left him with an oversized chest, a pink balding head, and a flushed face the color of boiled shrimp as he sat in a living room armchair, sucking air with raspy gasps.

An exception was Cousin André. Burly and strong, he loved to roam outdoors in the country when he visited us from Los Angeles. At sundown, I trailed behind him—when he was seventeen, I was six—as he pursued his favorite sport during his summer visits to the country: walking along the vineyard until he sighted through the scope of my father's bolt-action .22 a jackrabbit upright between two rows of grapevines, a stationary gray sentinel against the rosy sky. The rifle cracked, the rabbit flopped, and Cousin André moved to the next row in search of another prey. I'd never previously seen anyone killing and abandoning animals in this way—it was simply shooting, not hunting—and I chalked it up to a city boy's not knowing any better, although I did long for the day when I'd be allowed to look through the crosshairs of a rifle.

One summer afternoon, as I walked out on the grass near the blooming pink hydrangea bushes in front of our house, where we lived with my grandfather, I heard a voice call my name. I glanced toward the vineyard across the road, then swiveled toward the apricot orchard to the side of the house. No one was in sight. I again heard the disembodied voice. I don't recall how many times my name was called before I looked up to see, casually slung out on a high sycamore limb, Cousin André, relaxed and smiling from such an impossible height that I couldn't comprehend how he'd managed to climb so high—the distance between limbs appeared too great. But there he was, almost miraculously stretched out, resting among a jigsaw pattern of sycamore leaves and branches, blue sky above, instantly heroic to me in his achievement. From such a height, who knew what he could see?

Back in L.A. when he was eighteen and a crack mechanic in the Naval Air Reserve (the base commander would let no one else work on his airplane), Cousin André came down with polio and spent the rest of his life in a wheelchair. Paralyzed from the waist down with a weakened upper body, he had enough strength in his arms to slide himself on a board from his wheelchair into a specially rigged car he could steer, brake, and accelerate with his hands. With the board he could also get himself from his bed to the wheelchair, and he could cook, bathe, dress, and use the toilet by himself. When he was thirty-three, he married Barbara Gilmore. For twenty-five years he worked from home for Iskenderian Racing Cams, giving advice to hot-rod and race-car customers over a phone cradled between his shoulder and ear while flipping through manuals with his left hand and writing with his right.

The only times I remember seeing him again in the valley were at the drag races. He'd formed a car club with fellow polio victims and other disabled men called the "Kreepin Krips." They brought a '32 open-wheel Ford dragster to the valley races. With his legs shriveled, his chest and shoulders still big to my eyes, and his arms strong, he smiled and chatted cheerfully with me as he did that day from the heights of the sycamore. He thought he wouldn't live to fifty, but he didn't become completely incapacitated until he was fifty-four. He then needed constant care and a hoist to be moved from his wheelchair until he died seven days before his seventy-fifth birthday. He'd been married to Barbara forty-one years. When he was in bed dying, his cousin Tim pulled a souped-up '88 Chevy Cobra into the driveway and revved up the engine to prompt André's face into a smile.

That's how I remember him, as an astonishing boy with a sweet smile, though I recall him not amid hot rods or L.A. freeways, but in the country, looking down on me from a tremendously high tree, where he comes to mind with mythic dimensions every time I hear the biblical story of how "Zacchaeus ran on ahead and climbed up into a sycamore in order to see Him, for He was about to pass that way."

Uncle Fernand and Aunt Louise

André's parents, the ever-cheerful Uncle Fernand and Aunt Louise Rouseyrol, worked as pharmacists in the Los Angeles French Hospital, their long careers dating back to when pharmaceutical shelves still contained leeches, floating in bottles until dispensed with a doctor's prescription. The perfect great-aunt and great-uncle, they happily let me roam around L.A. on my own when I visited them, even when I was only eleven. I went solo to matinées at Grauman's Chinese Theater to watch Westerns like *Broken Arrow* and *Broken Lance* and to stare at the indentations of movie stars' feet and hands, as well as Betty Grable's leg, in concrete outside the theater, urban fossils I found drab in the Southern California sun and less inspiring than the pollywogs I saw sprouting tiny legs in ranch ditches. I roamed by myself into magic stores, unable to buy more than a trick fountain pen or whoopee cushion. In the evening I watched TV, still an amazingly uncommon gadget, not yet in our valley home.

One of the mysteries emerging for me at this time was my connection to these city relatives in terms of what I might share with them in temperament. Uncle Fernand, reminiscent of a stylish Adolphe Menjou with his dapper mustache, was quite jolly and loved to tell the story of the sunfish we caught when he took me to Millerton Lake during one of his valley visits, an event so out of keeping with his urban life that it expanded into the equivalent of an adventurous safari he had to recount every time I saw him. Aunt Louise, who was my grandfather's sister, shared her husband's jollity in the evening as she laughed at the antics of Gorgeous George, Bobo Brazil, and the Amazing Moolah, professional wrestlers I saw for the first time on TV in their West Hollywood home. She gleefully teased me whenever her beloved Los Angeles Dodgers beat my San Francisco Giants. Whether the high-spirited, energetic similarity between my aunt and uncle was due to the coincidence or influence of marriage I didn't know, but I did know that I shared blood with my aunt, so why she differed radically from her brother and sister, Uncle Lawrence and Aunt Marguerite, who also lived in L.A., astonished me. The extremes of merriment and gloom dealt to my uncles and aunts in unequal measure—I saw my grandfather as neutral—fascinated me.

Aunt Marguerite and Uncle Lawrence

Uncle Lawrence and Aunt Marguerite lived together on North Cherokee Avenue in Hancock Park, not far from where my grandfather and great-grandfather had farmed when they leased the La Brea Ranch in Hollywood from Mrs. Hancock. Both Lawrence and Marguerite maintained luxuriant dark hair into old age. Neither ever married. "Of course, they didn't have gray hair," other relatives griped; "they never married or had kids." Uncle Lawrence had a mysterious, longtime, never-seen-by-me girlfriend named Ethel, who I heard other relatives plaintively bring up along with the refrain "I don't know why he won't marry Ethel." Aunt Marguerite once told me why she hadn't married. I stood at her sink washing dishes during a visit to her house when I was in college, and she said, "I've always hated washing dishes. Even as a little girl I hated it, and I told my mother, 'I'm never going to get married because I'm not going to grow up and wash dishes.' And I didn't."

Both Uncle Lawrence and Aunt Marguerite shared a gloominess about the world that seemed to descend, at least in part, through the genes of their mother, my great-grandmother, Marie Jeanne Noussitou, who lived with them silently until her death at eighty-four, though to me she looked a hundred and four. I remember my great-grandmother as a tiny woman, almost monkey-like in the shape her face assumed with her hair severely pulled back, speaking, when she did speak, only French or Béarnaise, the Gascon dialect of her native Béarn. In old photos, her husband, François Bergon, contrasts with her tininess; a huge man with a scruffy walrus mustache, his burliness imposes itself in photos even when he's hunched in a chair, the ubiquitous cigar dangling between his stained fingers. A family story is that he put his dead cigar on a nightstand when he went to sleep and in the morning reached out and lit the stub before getting out of bed.

Uncle Lawrence also puffed on big cigars. Imposingly tall and broad-chested, with thick hair, horn-rimmed glasses, a flattened nose like a boxer's though he didn't box, he was the dapper city man in stylish hats and double-breasted suits, who dealt in real estate and was called by family and friends "Dudley." An old photo of my grandfather and other workers in a hayfield shows Uncle Lawrence in a black buggy hooked up to a horse he must have driven from town. In contrast to my grandfather in overalls, Uncle Lawrence sports a black hat, suit, and tie, and holds a black horsewhip.

He loved to hunt ducks and showed up at my grandfather's ranch in the fall when the season opened. One of the times he didn't arrive was in 1925 when he took a trip to Florida to check out real estate possibilities and wrote my grandfather, "I do not expect to be over to your place for duck season." He went on to say he would probably spend the winter in Miami to see if there was money to be made. He knew quite a few fellows from California who'd already made a lot of money. "They expect this winter to be the best one in the history of Florida," he wrote. He'd brought his shotgun with him to Miami because "they tell me that the ducks & geese are here in the winter by the millions."

Nevertheless, there was still a possibility of his coming to the ranch by way of Chicago, Kansas City, Denver, and San Francisco in time to hunt with my grandfather. "In case I should decide to come," he wrote, "I will send you a telegram to that effect. I sure would like to be there for the opening."

Uncle Lawrence was a talker, in contrast to my grandfather, who was a listener. A note of complaint tinged his monologues, creating a kind of discordant conversational music I found fascinating and identified with urban wheeler-dealers.

One Saturday morning, when I was seven, I sat in the doorway of the ranch butcher shop in order to overhear him bemoaning the current condition of something or other, while my grandfather in stocky, silent solidity resembled the butcher's block at which he worked, occasionally nodding while chopping with a meat cleaver. A cat sidled up to me and I petted it as a way to indicate my attention was elsewhere than snooping on their conversation, when I heard Uncle Lawrence tell my grandfather, "All kids today want to do is play with cats." I found this remark so ridiculously absurd I broke out laughing, which merited his gruff rejoinder, "What the hell do you think is so funny?"

When I was twelve and beginning to fashion my career as a future magician and escape artist, I challenged adult visitors to tie me up with fifty feet of soft clothesline I happened to have on hand. I would then retreat to the living room coat closet before emerging triumphantly freed.

Meeting the challenge with considerable irritation, Uncle Lawrence wrapped the rope several times around my neck before jerking my head back and forcing me to kneel while he cinched my bound wrists to my ankles behind my back. He winced with exertion, his boxer's face and flat nose like those of the old heavyweight champ Jess Willard.

"Jeez, what are you doing?" Aunt Marguerite asked with modulated alarm.

"He wanted to be tied up," Uncle Lawrence explained, as he put a finishing loop around my neck and knotted it snug enough to cut off much of my ability to breathe.

I managed to roll into the dark closet, and though it took longer than usual, I stepped out, released, free, contemptuously holding loose coils of rope in my extended hand. I saw a flash of surprise on my uncle's face and, for the first time, at least directed at me, something reminiscent of a smile.

"Jeez" was the usual exclamation opening Aunt Marguerite's critical response to the day's exemplification of world decline. She griped about our local priest's lousy hick sermon she'd talked her way through on a Sunday morning while visiting us. She found offense in the irritating way young girls dressed, but most offensive were L.A. politicians, notably Republicans, whose party adherents stretched through the agricultural valley to my Republican farming family. Her friendship and Democratic political allegiance with our bachelor cousin Henry brought them together to take brief vacation trips to Las Vegas. Despite what others saw as her oddness and irritability, I was immensely fond of her, probably because she was so fond of me. In her fascinating old-fashioned Hollywood home, furnished similarly to homes I later saw in Béarn, I encountered a strange world where people drank Arrowhead water from a bottled dispenser in the kitchen. The clear liquid sparkling in the upside-down five-gallon bottle of thick glass became a precious magical potion, in contrast to what readily gushed from pumps and flowed in canals and ditches in the valley. Aunt Marguerite read to me strange stories about an elephant named Babar, whose situation and concerns in a foreign country I could never quite get the hang of.

For decades, not knowing how to drive, she took public transportation to her clerk's job at the Los Angeles Department of Roads, an occupation allowing her an insider's view of political chicanery and human depravity. Her high opinion of the importance of education led to a cherished notion of professors as having wonderful careers, not aware, I'm sure, of Woodrow Wilson's claim that he found politics as a university president far worse than later as U.S. president. Her tribute to my own education came when she took a transcontinental train from L.A. to Boston to attend my college graduation, the only relative beside my parents to show up. She was sixty-five at the time and told me she was going to learn how to drive. Only Cousin Eddie in our family had the good temperament to successfully teach her.

When she was eighty-two, still possessing marvelous dark hair sweeping up from her forehead, she picked me up in her car at the Bonaventura Hotel, where I was attending the 1982 Modern Language Association convention, and drove us on surface roads—she never took freeways—to our regular lunch spot at Les Frères Taix, a longtime favorite restaurant of my family and other L.A. Béarnais. I had the day's special of beef tongue ecarlate for $3.55.

In the course of conversation, I asked Aunt Marguerite about the places she'd lived when she was growing up, and she mentioned the old Bergon family home on Melrose and Vine. "It's still there," she said.

Stunned and delighted, I asked, "Can we drive by?"

"Oh, do you really want to see that old thing?"

That afternoon, past and present collided for me when on the busy Hollywood intersection, next to Yum Yum Donuts, towered the two-story, wood-frame farmhouse, where her father—my great-grandfather—had moved his family to the dirt crossroads of Melrose and Vine after retiring from farming in 1917. I felt a magical connection to all my L.A. relatives. "This is great," I said.

"Jeez," Aunt Marguerite said, "let's go."

I I

In the Valley

The Displaced Béarnais

Cousin Henry didn't look like a stereotypical valley rancher. Swarthy and lean, ruggedly handsome with a lantern jaw, long nose, big ears, cropped black hair, and intense dark eyes, he looked in a photograph he sent me from those years like a strong peasant farmer in the Pyrenees without his beret. "Note on the picture," he wrote, "the cigar I am smoking, your father gave me." In the photo, he stands next to his seated mother, who looks like an ancient European grandmother in a dark shapeless dress, though she's only fifty-four. I sit on her knees, her hand cradling my chest. I'm seven and glower at the camera. Cousin Henry is twenty-nine. The expression I read in his stony face is one of resignation and dismay because he didn't expect to live long. "My mother couldn't have a baby normally," he told me. As a result, Cousin Henry was born prematurely at six months. The doctor told his mother, "He'll never make it." All through the years I knew him that remained Cousin Henry's bedrock belief: He wasn't going to make it. He didn't have long to live.

To call him simply "Cousin Henry" was a way for us to cut through the confusions of relationship: he was younger than my father, yet his father was the brother of my Béarnais great-grandmother. Cousin Henry was a bachelor—an only child—living on a ranch in Sanger with his parents—Uncle Louie and Aunt Marie—who on a Sunday at our place or theirs would argue in French about politics, religion, or farm prospects. Through Aunt Marie's heavily accented English, I picked up on her favorite harangue about how terribly the Church had treated Jeanne d'Arc. Cousin Henry, as a vigorous Democrat, faced off against the rest of my Republican ranching family. He was pretty much a loner, considered an odd duck—"I don't think he ever had a date," my father told me—but at the same time he was sharp, the only farmer in our family who played the stock market.

When Cousin Henry was fourteen and came down with rheumatic fever during his first year in high school, another doctor also declared he wouldn't make it. Despite his illness, his father made him work in the hay on their Selma ranch. During one attack when he was fifteen—his father could hear Henry's heart pounding—the doctor said he had a leaky valve and would be dead in forty-eight hours. The doctor could do nothing more for him. That winter Henry's father found an old country doctor who advised getting rid of the morphine and other medicine Henry had been taking for the past twelve months and to sit out in the winter sun behind the raisin sweatboxes. This doctor prescribed one medicine: digitalis. Two months later Henry recovered. That summer he was again mowing hay with horses. He never finished high school.

"This doc who saved me," Cousin Henry said, "told me don't go out at night and if you marry—if you do—watch your sex life. Sex is the hardest thing on a man's heart. And that's what I did. I didn't marry because I didn't want to leave behind a woman and kids." He did, however, smoke cigarettes for thirty-four years.

When Cousin Henry was fifty-five, he passed blood twice and was told by a doctor that if he passed blood a third time it would be cancer. He wanted to make a trip to his parents' birthplace in Béarn before he died. Years earlier he'd left the ranch after a rift with his father who'd wrongly blamed him for a broken axle on a tractor that cost a hundred dollars to fix. Henry was working in a Fresno paint store and told his boss, as an excuse to get time off, that he intended to go to France to look for a wife. Figuring he had at most five or six years left to live, he prepaid for his funeral and bought a steel casket and a cemetery plot with a concrete casing.

At the time of his trip, both of his parents were dead. Both had emigrated from Béarn, and both were born to Béarnais fathers and Basque mothers, according to Henry, but saw themselves only as French Béarnais. His mother intended to leave her home in Arette when she was eighteen, but the First World War delayed her arrival in the United States until she was twenty-two. She worked in San Francisco and Berkeley as a professional seamstress. "She could make pants from scratch," Henry said. Two years later Marie Lahourcade married Louis Noussitou, who'd just put in a windmill on virgin land in the San Joaquin Valley near Selma. He'd arrived from Feas in the Barétous Valley at the turn of the twentieth century when he was eighteen and worked on Southern California ranches. "He was an immigrant who spoke French," Henry said. "He got a lot of abuse from ranch cowboys." After a half-dozen years as a cowboy and ranch laborer, he was able to buy his own land. "When my father was twenty-four," Henry told me, "your grandfather was eighteen and took him to a whorehouse in Los Angeles." Henry reflected on the significance of his father's urban adventure. "He learned how a woman worked."

When he was sixty-eight, Cousin Henry went back to farming and owned an orange grove in Visalia. "If I live another year and a half," he told me at the time, "I'll have lived as long as my mother." As for living as long as his father, who'd reached seventy-eight, he saw no hope. Prostate and bladder trouble forced him out of bed ten to twelve times a night to pee. High blood pressure plagued him. "I don't want to reach the point of not being able to take care of myself," he said. Dieting had lowered his cholesterol to 170, and although the doctor wanted it down to 150, he intended to get as low as 160 and quit.

Since he never knew when he might die, he sold his ranch when he was seventy-three and moved into The Hacienda, once a fancy 1950s motel on old Highway 99 outside Fresno, converted into a retirement home with a communal dining room. "I'm just waiting to kick the bucket," he told me at the time. He'd always thought his heart would give out, but after a physical he learned from a doctor that his heart, with a pulse of fifty, was the strongest thing he had. At seventy-eight, Cousin Henry realized that in a few months he would have lived as long as his father. "I'll beat him," he said.

With a few shirts and pants on wire hangers in his small Hacienda room, Cousin Henry reminded me of those immigrant Greek bachelors that my friend Zeese Papanikolas has written about, men who came from the old country to find work in the West, men who press lightly on the world. Henry didn't want to be a burden on others. He still worried about reaching the point of not being able to take care of himself.

After seven years in The Hacienda, he began running short of money and moved to a smaller, cheaper one-bedroom apartment in the Link Care Center in Fresno, a Christian-sponsored senior center, where he prepared his own meals. He was eighty. "I never thought I'd live this long," he told me. "I only have a few thousand left, and when that's gone I'll go on welfare," a prospect he found both unbelievable and shameful. On an electric hot plate Henry warmed up Campbell's Pork & Beans but lived mostly on cans of fruit cocktail and Rite Aid Nutritional Drink, bought by the case. When we went for a Basque dinner at the Santa Fe Hotel, he didn't want soup but after the big bowl arrived he took seconds. After devouring half a large T-bone with his new dentures, he complained that the steak was getting tough. He turned his attention to extra helpings of potato salad and stewed string beans. Henry eyed the young waitress who'd been talking to me and as she walked away, he said, "I think that girl would marry you, if you were single."

He began sending me somewhat paranoid notes about the welfare people who checked on him. In flusher times, Henry had sold some stock to give loans to my aunt and father, and I now gave him some money, which he initially refused but later accepted when it was couched as a loan. He accepted a few checks until one I'd sent him came back to me in an envelope. "Dear Cousin," he wrote. "Thank you for the check, but I am returning it on account of the welfare people that come here. Don't come see me." On the phone he told me he'd destroyed the photographs of us at Millerton Lake and at the Table Mountain Casino, where we'd spent the afternoon playing the slots. He'd also cut me out of a photo taken at the Basque Hotel, though he'd left Holly in. He didn't want welfare to hound me for money.

"I never thought I'd sink this low," he said the next time I visited him. He'd grown a beard, the gaunt hollows of his eyes had deepened, and a sweet-sour odor hung on his breath. He ate ravenously when we went out for dinner. After chowing down on a plate of tender, braised lamb shanks at a small Armenian restaurant, Henry exclaimed, "What a blowout!" With his usual precise memory for detail and dates, he talked about our family in the San Joaquin Valley. During the Depression his father had worked off the farm, driving horse-drawn land scrapers for other ranchers, and his mother didn't get her first refrigerator and washing machine until she was forty-one. My grandmother, on the other hand, had an indoor bathroom, and my grandfather acquired several ranches during the Depression. "He got real big real quick," Henry said, "and he had the newest things." At one time, Henry recalled, my grandfather had a 1926 personal touring car. When my grandmother died, my grandfather owned a new Plymouth, and in 1945 when he was on a hunting trip, his second wife took off in his new Dodge. "Too bad you couldn't have kept that land in the family," Henry said about my grandfather's ranch. "One of you," he added, meaning my brother or me, "could've been a farmer. Your father was a farmer. He sure came to a bad end."

I received a call from the chaplain of the senior center saying how one day Henry couldn't get out of bed and after being diagnosed with pneumonia he'd been transferred to Pacific Gardens Nursing and Rehabilitation Center, where luckily a room had become available. The chaplain, who'd spent forty years as a missionary in Rwanda and Burundi, greatly enjoyed getting to know Henry, he told me, and even identified with him as a father figure since his own father had died and was buried before he could return from Africa. Henry had warned the chaplain, "I was born a Catholic and I'll die a Catholic," but the chaplain assured him, "Henry, I just want you to love Jesus and to know that he loves you and that you have eternal life."

When I arrived at the senior center to clean out Henry's apartment and to sort through the clothes he would need at the nursing home, the chaplain told me that he'd already transferred Henry's billfold, insurance papers, and a couple of photographs to the nursing home. He wanted me to open Henry's small safe-deposit box. It was empty. The chaplain had found a handsome photo of Henry when he was about twenty and pinned it up on the bulletin board next to his bed in the nursing home, thinking it would perk him up. When we arrived at the home, the photo was gone, and the chaplain, greatly disappointed, asked where it went. In return, Henry asked, "Is that picture important to you?" Henry then turned his attention to the TV news about some California propositions proposed for the next election.

A year later, two weeks before the general election, a nurse and I helped Henry out of bed and I pushed him into the lobby in a wheelchair. At eighty-three, he'd reached the point of not being able to take care of himself, although nothing specific had been found wrong with him, even by "those guys who stick their fingers up your butt," he said. "Twenty-five years ago, I was pissing blood. Now my piss is all right. I don't like them putting their fingers up your butt." He turned toward the TV in the lobby and its talk of the upcoming presidential election. "I sure hope Bush gets licked," he said. "I want to be here two more weeks and then I don't care what happens to me. If that knucklehead Bush gets licked, I'll die happy."

We looked at some of the photos he'd kept—one of his mother, two snapshots of himself (one from an automatic photo booth, probably taken for his passport, another of us at the Basque Hotel with me scissored out), a photo of a cousin in France, and another of a large French farmhouse with Henry's writing on the back, "Noussitou homestead Feas," the ancestral home he'd visited under the guise of finding a wife. "My mom or dad never said anything about me getting married," he said, "until right before he died my father told me, 'Henry, we're not going to be here forever. Aren't you looking around for a wife?' Ten days later my father died."

I asked Henry, "Did you ever have sex with a woman?"

"No," he replied, "I never have. I've never told anyone that before." He thought for a bit. "To be honest with you, I never was really woman crazy."

During my visit to his room when he was eighty-seven, a few months before he died, he was sleeping and I didn't wake him. I thought about what might have been different with his life if his parents hadn't had to immigrate to America, and if Henry could have lived on the Noussitou farm in the beautiful, green

Barétous Valley. When I visited my relatives there, they showed
me a framed photograph of Henry's grandfather, Jean Pierre
Noussitou, who was my great-great-grandfather. Jean Pierre had
been the mayor of Feas for thirty years, my relatives said. "He
had a lot of politics but no money." On his chest hung a medal
commemorating his military service for Napoleon III during
the Franco-Prussian War. He'd given the medal to his son Louis
when he went to America. Louis passed it on to his son, Henry,
who gave it to me.

One afternoon in the Oloron-Sainte-Marie town square,
near the charcuterie owned by my relatives, I saw old men in
Béarnais berets happily chatting with each other—about what?—
most likely politics, religion, farm prospects, family history—and
I imagined how easily Henry would fit in, how much he looked
like these men, and how to my eye he would appear more at
home here than in the San Joaquin Valley on his father's alkali
farm or in a Fresno paint store or in a Highway 99 senior center.
Many immigrants would've been happier in their homeland and
not coming West.

"I'm a Frenchman," Henry told me when I'd asked him about
the food in the nursing home. "I like French food, the way a
German likes German food, but not this food." In the photograph I'd taken of him after a family-style dinner at the boarders'
table in the Basque Hotel, back when he was eighty-one, Henry
had flashed an uncharacteristically big smile, intentionally so, he
said at the time, to show off his new dentures. Years later, when
we looked at the photo, he said in his tone of typical regret, "If
I'd died a few years earlier, I would've had most of my teeth."

King of the San Joaquin

No one better fit the role of the tough, optimistic Western rancher than Short Watson, but everyone thought his life might be as short as his name suggested, given how hard he drank, dipped snuff, smoked cigars, gambled, and worked during his valley ranching days. He did almost die from a heart attack after a Thanksgiving Day get-together, when he was eighty-two, but luckily he was at a card table in a nearby casino, equipped with a defibrillator and a nurse on call who knew how to work it. After eight days Short became conscious in a hospital bed, still groggy, as his family explained what had happened at the card table and his grandson added, "You had a good hand, too, Pappy." Short quickly brightened and responded, "Did you get the money?" Doctors implanted a cardioverter defibrillator in his chest. Short explained to me how it worked. "If my heart stops again, it's supposed to shock it alive." Amusement at this idea prompted his habitual response to events: a glint in the eye and barrel-chested, rumbling laughter. "So I guess I'll live forever."

I met Short in the San Joaquin Valley, during a summer when my cousin and I drove harobeds in a hay-hauling business for a Russian farmer. Short also had latched on to these new machines for gathering and stacking hay bales, advertising himself in *The Madera Tribune* as "The Harobed King of the San Joaquin." How he had time to run this sideline business, farm his own land, and drink and gamble in the bars became apparent in the huge presence he cast in the advertisement photograph: posed in front of a new harobed, wearing Levi's and a battered muleskinner's hat, his shirt pocket packed with a tin of Copenhagen and cigars, he stood with the big chest and hard belly of old-time strong men, ready to work. In one year, he hauled nearly a million bales. When I introduced him to Darrell Winfield, the future Marlboro Man shook Short's large hand and said, "You have the biggest hands of any man I've ever met."

Asked how he got to be called "Short," he said, "I think it was some damn neighbors when I was a kid." They pinned him with the diminutive moniker when he was five years old in the Imperial Valley, where he was born, and the name stuck because, as he explained, "I was short and fat until I was about fifteen, before I got any height. Half the people in Madera don't know my real name." He shared his real name, Henry, with his dad, who'd come to California from Longview, Texas, in 1911, and worked in Hollywood as a movie location scout and prop man. His father kept a vegetable garden in Hollywood where Paramount Studio now stands. Short's mother talked about seeing Charlie Chaplin make hats fly around a movie set. Short's father was on a hunt for a cowboy movie location for Universal Studios when he saw cotton growing beautifully in the Imperial Valley and decided he wanted to farm as he had back in Texas. That's what Short also said he wanted to do after his family moved to Madera County. While delivering a speech in front of his eighth-grade class at Ripperdan Elementary School on the topic of what-I-want-to-be-when-I-grow-up, Short declared, "I want to be a farmer."

During the Depression, as a teenager, Short worked on a dairy farm near the San Joaquin River for thirty dollars a month, plus room and board, and then drove tractors for three dollars a day on a Sacramento Valley farm of grain, sugar beets, and beans. He was back in Madera County milking cows on the Stage Ranch, which he would one day own, when the Second World War broke out and he said, "I'm out of here." Twenty days after Pearl Harbor was attacked, he enlisted in the navy and volunteered for sea duty. First, though, he was at the Oakland air base and then in Livermore, where they bussed in girls from Mills College for weekend dances. "Those were good times," he said.

Trained as a navy butcher, he spent twenty-two months in the South Pacific on a support ship for seaplanes. When he learned that my father-in-law had flown amphibious PBYs for the naval air force in the South Pacific, Short said, "I bet he came on our ship"—the USS *Chandeleur* (AV-10)—"or our sister ship, though it got shot up a little bit." Holly's father once thought his plane wasn't going to make it while trying to take off from the water in a storm on the China Sea. "We were all through there," Short said, "Saipan, Okinawa. I saw some of those PBYs knock the pontoons off the wings when trying to land. Pilots stayed the night on our ship and called PBYs 'cracker boxes.' They were about right, too."

Down in the ship's hold, sailors dealt blackjack on waist-high projectile crates used as tables. An American Indian sailor named Jack Jackson stealthily snapped the keys off the belt of the storekeeper during a game and sneaked away to make an imprint of the keys on a bar of soap. A duplicate key allowed Short and others to steal beer from the officers' locker and toss the cans of Miller's High Life over the side. "That Indian boy was petty officer first class but didn't care if he got busted because he said he'd be chief when he returned to the rez." Short was rated petty officer second class and about ready for first class when he got busted, accused of making raisin jack, though he had nothing to do with that operation. "They shanghaied me," he said. "I wouldn't squeeze on the guy." He never got caught for the booze he was really cooking, called Pink Lady.

As the USS *Chandeleur* sailed into San Francisco Bay after nearly two years at sea, Bank of America sent out a boat to sell traveler's checks to the sailors before they reached harbor. Short's pay had started at twenty dollars a month but rose to fifty with an additional twenty percent for sea duty. His real income, though, came from shooting craps. "That's how I bought my first ranch," he said. He saved some winnings to blow on shore, but with the rest he bought seven thousand dollars' worth of traveler's checks, which he sent to his dad for a down payment on a ranch. After five and a half years in the navy, Short was back in the San Joaquin Valley on thirty acres with twenty dairy cows.

Cesare Pierini was the banker in Madera who helped farmers in those days. "Goddamn, Cesare, I need some more cows," Short told him. A dairy was selling out the next day. As Short tells the story, the banker responded, "Goddamn, Watson, what you got to mortgage? We've got nothing to put on paper." The cows Short owned were already mortgaged. "If the examiners come around," Cesare explained, "and they see money out and no collateral I'll get in a big bunch of trouble." Short says he knew Cesare was going to give him the loan, he just didn't know how he was going to do it. "I'll tell you what, Watson," Cesare said, "you go buy the cows you want. Beat the check back here with the bill of sale, and we'll mortgage *those* cows."

Short had to go into Dearborn Hospital in Madera for a hernia operation. "That's where I met Margaret," he said about Margaret Long, his future wife, who worked for Doctor Swift. "So I was unconscious when I met my wife." Short took on an additional job as herdsman for a nearby dairy with five hundred cows, making five hundred dollars a month. "Lots of money in those days," he said. "I'd milk my cows at midnight and noon and be at the other ranch at two in the morning and two in the afternoon." Margaret washed the machines between milkings and took care of their two sons, Larry and Don. They moved back up north to a ranch near Chico in the early 1950s, where their daughter Edie was born, before moving back to Madera County and a dairy partnership on the Stage Ranch with 625 acres, 120 cows, and another daughter, Cindy. In the 1960s, Short sold the Stage Ranch and bought a fifty-acre vineyard and ranch house near where my family lived. He was also offered a 900-acre ranch at a good deal, if he would put a lien on his home place. "I should've took it, but it was a hell of a gamble."

He gambled in other ways, flopping dice cups at Rose's, or gambling in the back room of Malick's bar or downtown at the Ritz, though he says about the poker players at the Ritz, "I couldn't beat those boys there." He preferred the game at the Mission Bar. He won the money for his first pickup on the Stage Ranch from his friend Hart Nelson in a game at Malick's. "I bet him head-up one night. He gave me a check for twelve hundred dollars, and I went down and got me a new pickup for sixteen hundred. Hart was a good sport." One morning, when Short went over to Hart's house to buy some cows, Hart stumbled from bed and asked his wife, Mary, to bring him a drink. She filled a glass with liquor. "One of those big water glasses," Short said, "I guess it was bourbon—Early Times, I think." Hart looked up at Mary and said, "What's the matter, honey? What are you trying to do, wean me? Don't you love me anymore?" Short laughed at the memory. "Hart was funny. Strong as a bull, too. I liked that old boy." Hart was killed when he rolled his car while driving from one of the two bars he bought after selling his ranch.

Short's brother-in-law, Bob Smith, had years earlier worked as a longtime ranch foreman for my grandfather, and after my grandfather's death Short leased the ranch from my dad. Our ranch bordered fields owned by Sherman Thomas, who originally migrated penniless from Faulkner County, Arkansas, worked as a janitor, and eventually became one of the biggest ranchers in Madera County and the central San Joaquin Valley. His workers used tractors to shave the bank of Cottonwood Creek when the water was high so that our ranch would get flooded instead of his. "That's when I got your dad excited," Short said. "I took the fourteener and the scraper down there and was cutting the bank where we had only eighteen acres. I was going to flood Sherman, but your dad stopped me. It was probably good because he could've sued your dad instead of me."

Later Sherman put armed guards on Cottonwood Creek. "I never did like the old fucker too well. He flooded me too many times." Nevertheless, Sherman later called and asked Short to manage his ranches. "He couldn't have paid me enough," Short said.

Around that time, Short put his own vineyard and farm equipment up for sale. I remember asking him why. He replied, "Why the fuck do I want a ranching empire?" He'd had enough land under lease to farm. At one point, he leased another ranch besides ours and farmed fifteen hundred acres of open ground in cotton and corn but mostly alfalfa. It hit me at the time how much Short loved the process of farming. On summer nights, when the cut-and-raked alfalfa was too dry to bale, he slept in the field with his hand on the windrow of alfalfa so he could feel the dew come in. With enough moisture in the hay so the leaves wouldn't shatter, he baled through the night until the morning heat dried out the hay again. I formulated an idea about work at the time: when you're doing in life what you think you were meant to do, that's when you get the gold ring.

After my father sold the ranch to two Armenian grape growers, they hired Short as ranch manager to plant and develop vineyards of six varietals—Carignan, Thompson, Colombard, Chenin Blanc, Grenash, and Barbera—all of which were sold to Gallo Winery, the biggest in California. "Julio Gallo was a crooked fucker," Short said. "You have to give him credit, though. The old boy was pretty smart. He knew how to control the market. He was so big and rich he could put his wine on the shelf and drop his price and break everyone else." He also controlled the price farmers received by determining the demand.

One day, Gallo's field man arrived on the ranch with Julio Gallo himself, who sat in the car when the field man climbed out to announce to Short, "Mr. Gallo doesn't want to buy any more Carignans."

"Fuck Gallo," Short hollered back. He saw the old man hunker down in the passenger seat.

"I pulled some pretty good ones on that old boy. He didn't want Carignans, but he got 'em."

Short picked the grapes at night with two mechanical pickers, one in the field of Carignans, the other in the field of Barbera vines. He mixed the Carignan berries with the similar-looking Barbera and sent them off to the winery.

"At the end of the year," Short said, "the girl in the Gallo office called me and said, 'Hey, Short, what did you do with them Carignans?' I told her, 'You know, a funny thing happened to those Carignans. They turned into Barbera overnight.'

"Later on," Short continued, "Gallo had a field man who was halfway honest, and when I told him what I did he just laughed."

After retiring, Short returned to familiar farm country in the northern Sacramento Valley, living not far from his daughter Edie, who raised quarter horses on a few acres outside Orland. The town and country reminded me of Madera County forty years earlier. During a year Holly and I were on sabbatical in Berkeley, Short threw a barbecue in Orland for my birthday, much like the old days in the San Joaquin Valley, when he hosted a reception at the ranch after my mother's death and a later party for Holly and me after we were married on the East Coast. In Orland, I went into a convenience store with him. The Pakistani worker behind the counter said to Short, "Hello, cowboy," and automatically reached for a can of Copenhagen. "I've been chewing it now for seventy-five years," Short said. He often gambled at the nearby Rolling Hills Casino, where he had his heart attack. "I've won enough and lost enough that they feed me up there. I've been pretty lucky. I don't lose more than I won the day before. This last month I'm fifteen thousand ahead."

To celebrate a birthday, he went with his daughter and two friends to Reno. One of the friends brought some bottles of wine, which he and Short finished off. "I was feeling pretty damn good," Short said, "and got into a card game." Blackjack. "I was betting five hundred, winning, losing, and I guess I was lucky. I was drinking brandy on top of that wine. I got so goddamn drunk they made me quit. So I went to bed. They put me to bed really. I woke up the next morning and the table at the side of the bed was full of chips."

He counted the chips and gave a thousand each to his daughter and two friends to cash out so the casino wouldn't get his Social Security number, put a final five hundred on the table, lost, and went home with four thousand dollars.

"Hey, Short," one of the friends asked him in town one day, "are you going back to Reno for your ninetieth birthday?"

"Damn right," Short said, "I'm going back for my ninetieth birthday and try again, but I ain't going to get that drunk."

When Short was ninety-three, he lived in a one-room cabaña next to the house of his younger daughter, Cindy, and his son-in-law Terence back in the San Joaquin Valley. He still dipped snoose—a can a day—but no longer drank. He now gambled at the Indian casinos in the hills. When running up a debt on a losing streak, he said with a laugh, "You have to entertain yourself." He considered moving into an assisted-living complex. "The problem is," he told me, "they're so damn expensive. If I move in now, I'll run out of money in three or four years."

I told him I'd be heading to Colorado in the fall rather than in the summer.

"You'll be there when the elk are migrating," he said.

"That's right," I said. "What we call Elk Hill is sometimes covered with migrating elk."

"Let me know when you get out there," he said, "and I just might hop on a plane and come and see you."

When I told a friend we knew in the San Joaquin Valley that Short would be ninety-five years old on his next birthday, the friend replied, "And who said drinking wasn't good for you?"

Rose in a Country of Men

Country women I knew who were no longer girls had become mostly wives on ranches taking care of their men and children. Their work was at home. Exceptions might be a nurse like my mother, or a schoolteacher like my aunt, who also worked outside the home in a mixed world of men and women. The only husbandless woman we knew working solely in the country of men was Rose.

Rose ran a bar south of town at a country crossroads in those years unceremoniously called Jap Corner. Kitty-corner from the bar was Hedeo and Keyo Mochizuki's store, and across the road stretched fields once owned by my grandfather called the Jap Corner Ranch. Men owned all the other bars in Madera County. Rose's was more properly a tavern, the place you went for both drinks and good food. An old rancher recently told me what everyone used to say: "That woman could sure cook."

Other women usually came into the bar for special occasions when Rose cooked in the evening for a group, something she also did when she catered outside events, such as my sister's wedding reception in the parish hall. Young girls on that day circulated among wedding guests with platters of chicken livers and water chestnuts wrapped in bacon. Rose's regular clientele, though, were men. At noon, ranchers, cattlemen, grape growers, cotton farmers, cowboys, irrigators, tractor drivers, construction workers, equipment salesmen, and even guys from town crammed into the bar for lunch.

Rose had luxuriant black hair sweeping high off her forehead and an expressive, queenly face, quick to laugh and just as quick to turn serious as she bantered with men or kept them in line. Now and then she'd have a helper behind the bar or in the kitchen, but she was the one in charge. No shot glass measured the booze she poured with a generous hand and a warm smile. Something about her unflappable manner and bearing gave her a regal dignity. I was a teenager when I got to know her. She was in her fifties, full-bodied, emanating both sexual vitality and motherly concern. She was a man's woman. Men liked her and she liked men.

When the cooking was over, she held court behind the bar. Stell Manfredi, who later became Madera county commissioner, remembers how as teenagers "Ken, Ray, and I used to drink at her place. Of course, we were underage. Later on in life, I spent copious hours talking to Rose about politics, life, and the American Way. She knew governors, local, state, and federal politicians and wasn't bashful about expressing her views."

We all heard lectures from her about American Western values, especially the importance of dignity and moral character. The way to win and hold someone's love was to be frank, simple, and honest. A real man who was a true Westerner always kept his word. Do too much for people and they do nothing for themselves. Everything pivots on soil and water. Ranchers and farmers sustain and nourish the world, although they're being reduced to an infinitesimal proportion of the population.

Through my own blurry view at the bar late at night, I saw Rose's brown eyes squint into a shooter's aim as her steady, mellifluous voice drove home a point with unflinching authority. As the view got blurrier, a free pickled egg might appear on a plate in front of me to counteract alcohol, a common belief about food in those years, allowing you to drink more. After a few pickled eggs, a piece of cold fried chicken might appear. "Here's where the eggs came from," Rose would say.

As the social disruptions of the 1960s cranked up, Rose's conservative views spread more frequently beyond the bar through letters to the editor of *The Madera Tribune* and *The Republican Newsletter*. She became a vocal member of many organizations and committees, like the Tax Payers Association and the Juvenile Justice Committee. In the bar, we learned how the election of Franklin D. Roosevelt brought about social security, welfare, and the laziness of man.

Rose later collected in a binder some fifty pages of short essays she wrote during this time as a member of the Madera Toastmistress Club and gave them to Stell, who helpfully handed them on to me for this sketch. Rose called these pieces her "short stories," and while three of them are stories with charming, personal details of her early life, most, as Stell told me, were "on subjects she pontificates on" under single-word topics assigned by the club president—Youth, Morals, Water, Farmers, Truth, etc.—all subjects we heard Rose forcefully expound upon in the bar.

The Madera City Council got a glimpse of Rose's forcefulness when she led a seventeen-month fight to save the town's seventy-seven-year-old water tower. As reported in the town newspaper, Rose told the council members, who were all men, "You people were voted here not to fight us but to fight for us." Then she put the mayor on notice, telling him if he didn't "cooperate, he may not be mayor next time. I'm going to tell you I won't forget it, and if I'm still around no one else will forget it either." The mayor sided with Rose and provided the swing vote for the city to fork over money to save the tower. Men in town were learning what we knew in the country: Don't mess with Rose.

In 1970, as chair of the Madera County Fair, Rose introduced Governor Ronald Reagan to the people of Madera. "As I was standing at the podium beside Governor Reagan," Rose later recalled, "a thought crossed my mind. How would my parents have felt if they could have known that such a special advantage would be granted their daughter?"

She was the daughter of Italian immigrants—Constantino Bini and Catarina Schiavani—and she was appropriately born on the Fourth of July on her parents' Madera farm in 1911, the same year as my mother, though Rose lived more than three decades longer, until she was ninety-six.

She identified her own early development with that of Madera County. The county was just eighteen years old when she was born, the same year the Madera water tower was built, giving townspeople, she wrote, "one of their very first luxuries, running water in their homes." Five years later, all the land on the west side of the county was owned by Miller & Lux, where many Italian immigrants came to work. "All of that land was developed with a two-horse Fresno Scraper," Rose wrote. The famous scraper, made of iron instead of wood and touted as one of the most important agricultural and civil engineering tools ever made, allowed for efficient construction of irrigation ditches and canals. My grandfather's Fresno scraper is in the Madera County Museum.

On her parents' farm Rose learned the value of good water and good soil. On the cattle company's westside land, she remembers seeing "the artesian well at the Bonita Ranch bubbling silently and gently out of the ground." Her family's equipment consisted of a plow, a cultivator, a revolving harrow, a pick, a shovel, and a hoe, the same tools, she said, that tamed Madera County. "This was the day of the drummer, with his little horse-drawn covered wagon, selling his wares." Basic clothes, groceries, and farm equipment were sold in town at the Rosenthal Kutner General Merchandise store, "the Wal-Mart of that day," but she remembered the other salesmen who came and "took orders for grocery staples that were shipped to us from San Francisco."

Traveling salesmen fascinated her. She recalled with excitement when they showed up. "The day of their arrival was a holiday."

"In the olden days," she wrote, "especially in Italian families, the children were automatically involved in assuming their duties and responsibilities toward the upkeep of the home." Boys worked in the fields, girls in the house. When she was quite young, Rose discovered she enjoyed cooking. "As I grew older," she wrote, "I began to dream about becoming a famous cook and that one day I would own my own great restaurant."

In 1928, when she was seventeen, she married twenty-six-year-old Natale Marchetti, who also came from a farming family. Born in Italy, Nat had arrived in the valley with his parents when he was a year old. Rose's father was dead, and the newlyweds moved in with Rose's mother and two brothers on the family farm west of Madera. "That was when I learned that our gains in life did not come easy," Rose later wrote. "Our Great Depression," as she called it, hit the following year, and she saw farmers who couldn't sell their crops and went bankrupt. She saw people "losing their jobs, their homes, their families falling apart. Suicides were frequent," she wrote. "I learned that the Depression was the most effective mathematics instructor that ever hit the college of hard knocks. One term in that class remains with you forever. The fear, the pain and the poverty were horrendous."

She and Nat realized they had to branch out from farming if they were to survive. They went to work for Krikor Arakelian, the Armenian immigrant fruit peddler who'd become a melon king and owner of Madera's Mission Bell Winery. Rose and Nat took over operation of the winery boardinghouse. Their day started at 5:00 a.m. cooking breakfast for the workers, followed by lunch preparation at 11:00 a.m. and dinner at 5:00 p.m. Besides cooking, Rose served meals, cleaned the kitchen, and washed dishes. Between meals, she helped Mrs. Arakelian at her home in what they called the Big House. Mrs. Arakelian had been born in Constantinople but had a similar first name: Rosa.

"After the day was complete," Rose remembered, "if there was any spare time, I would read. The reading consisted of cookbooks."

She discovered a corned beef recipe that sounded simple and good. After discussing it with Nat, they ordered the meat and had it simmering by 7:30 one morning. At 11:00, after finishing in the Big House, Rose drove back to the cookhouse, where Nat waited at the door with a two-prong fork in his hand. "As I got out of the car," Rose said, "he began to yell, scream, and wave the fork. He frightened me half to death."

She ran to the kettle to discover the corned beef had shrunk to a quarter of its original size. "I couldn't believe my eyes," she said. While still hollering at her, Nat stabbed at the little piece of meat with the fork but it was so tough it was like trying to spear a floating brick. It bounced against the sides of the kettle, splashing water all over the stove.

"It was the funniest thing I had seen," Rose said. "Oh, how I wanted to laugh, but I knew my life was in the balance." Nat was panic-stricken. "The thought of not having food for approximately fifty people made him lose all sense of reasoning. I finally got his attention and told him to go to the Jap store to get three boxes of those beautiful Noble wieners." Rose suspected that if Nat felt he'd had three minutes to spare he would have killed her first, but he turned and went to get the locally made wieners.

While he was gone Rose removed the corned beef and boiled the broth for cabbage, potatoes, and the wieners. When the lunch bell rang and the men filed into the dining room, "the table was laden with those beautiful wieners full of juice, the cabbage and potatoes done to perfection. The wieners saved the day and my life, to live on and continue to dream of the great restaurant that I would one day own."

After going on to run the kitchen for the Matthews Lumber Company at Green's Mill, Rose and Nat finally opened their own lunch counter and bar in March of 1943 at Jap Corner in the unincorporated community of Ripperdan. They named it the Farmer's Roundup, and though the name never officially changed, everyone called it "Rose's" after Nat died fourteen years later and Rose continued running the place alone for another thirty-five years.

Nat was only fifty-five when he died on Christmas Day in 1957, but he looked older. Rose, on the other hand, looked sprier than the nine years separating them. Once, when Nat got mad at her for flirting with guys at the bar while serving drinks, he retreated with a young friend to the house where he and Rose lived behind the tavern. The friend tried to calm Nat down by saying what a nice person Rose really was.

Nat hunched in his chair with his arms crossed, glaring back at his young friend. "Well," Nat said, emphasizing each word, "*she...can...cook*."

Rose's became a valley landmark as a fabulous place to eat. Pork chops, lamb chops, and steaks were always cooked stove-top in cast-iron skillets. I once asked her how she could make something so simple taste so good. "Get good meat," she told me, "salt it real well, and cook it just right"—a lesson easier to remember than execute, especially the "just right" part.

Apparently, though, Rose's place didn't fulfill her dream of owning a great restaurant. "It has been only recently," she would later write, "that I resigned myself to the truth. I would never own more than Rose's, a lunch counter in Ripperdan."

Three years after Nat's death, an incident in the bar illustrated Rose's view of "a real man." Her basic way of judging people coincided with the Old West adage: "I don't care what Sam says of Joe, it's what Joe does to me that counts. We're all here to get rich, and your dollar is as good as mine." Once, though, she made an error of judgment based on appearances and scuttlebutt.

A traveling construction crew moved into the Ripperdan district to build lateral canals for irrigation water from the San Joaquin River. The crew gathered in Rose's for after-work sandwiches and beer. She found the men "a great lot" of colorful wage earners, consisting of both Casanovas and Freeloaders.

"For them," Rose wrote, "life consists of motel rooms or a moving trailer," a rootless life punctuated by moments of communal living since they all gathered for jobs in the same motel or trailer court, some with families, others alone. "Mix-ups in families and love triangles are a continual event," she noted. "The women spend much of their time trying to keep watch on their roaming husbands, and most always fail."

One Casanova named John Quintana was a muscular, outdoor man with an enchanting voice. "He had all the charm and charisma that goes with a prowling man," Rose said. "He was handsome and he knew it."

In contrast, Joe Bench was small and shriveled, a bit weaselly, and loved to gamble but "because luck was not always with him, he acquired the title of 'freeloader.'" Rose never referred to him by that derogatory name because in reality, she said, he was kind, prompt in paying his loans, and a true gentleman. "To me," she wrote, "he was the personification of 'a real man,'" and yet "I knew I had subconsciously accepted him by the degrading label he carried. How mistaken I was!"

One evening the ladies' man John Quintana came into the bar earlier than usual and asked Rose to cook dinner for him. He hadn't been to work for three days. As he ate, Rose said, "he told me of his three-day escapade and the great chicks he had spent his time with. His true purpose in the world was to bring joy to those lucky women who had the good fortune to meet him.

"On and on he boasted," Rose said, and as "the crew began to drift in he proceeded to tell his story to all the guys." After a round of drinks, the bar was buzzing and the jukebox playing when John Quintana called out, "Rose, come around the bar and dance with me."

"I enjoyed dancing," Rose said, "and I accepted."

As they were swaying to the music, Rose recalled, "I was facing the front window and I noticed a tall, stately, and handsome Amazonian-type girl go by." Rose hadn't seen her before, but John whirled her around and was facing the window. "I felt John's knees buckle, and I then knew who the girl was."

The woman walked into the bar, and John introduced Rose to his wife. "Knowing he had not been home for three days," Rose said, "I knew she was going to blame me and probably slap me under the table."

The bar went icily silent, with thirty-five men not saying a word. "Where had all the conversation gone?" Rose wondered. "Everyone was staring at the three of us on the floor."

In that moment, Joe Bench, recognizing Rose's embarrassment, banged his hand on the bar and said, "Rose, hurry up, pour the next round. You know the next dance is on me."

Joe had never previously asked Rose to dance and never asked again during the rest of the time the crew worked in the district, but that evening they danced. "He saved my day!" Rose recalled years later. "I had never had the pleasure to see a man stand so tall."

As a man's woman she said things shocking to those of us in our teens and early twenties under the growing influence of changing attitudes toward ethnic minorities and women. Stell remembers talking to Rose about a guy hitting a woman, and he told her, "There's no reason to hit a woman unless she's coming at you with a knife." Rose replied, "Sometimes they need to be slapped around."

Just as shocking to some of us was her late-night lecture about how to vote in an upcoming election because "you don't want a Mexican telling you what to do." In theory, Rose knew the immigrant story of those, as she described them, "who toiled and broke every inch of the untouched, virgin soil, which surrounds Madera today"—Italians like her own family, Armenians like the Arakelians she worked for, also Croatians, French, Portuguese, Swedes, Russians, Basques, and others who were once, she wrote, "the young immigrants, that then, like now, were searching to fulfill their dreams of a new world that might have held for them a promise of a new future."

Those immigrants of the California Dream, whose children and grandchildren came into her bar, were mostly European, or early Californios, like my buddy Ronnie Preciado's great-grandfather Ygnacio, who emigrated from Mexico to California in the 1860s, and his great-grandmother, Adelaida, born in California in 1852, both living in Madera and listed as white in the 1900 federal census, as was their son who was the county tax collector in 1907 and another who owned a store on the main street in 1912. At that time the law allowed only whites and blacks of African descent to become naturalized citizens. Other people of so-called color—brown or yellow or red—were excluded on the basis of their race.

Rose didn't acknowledge recent Mexicans as part of the same immigrant dream she extolled when talking about her own relatives. In 1965, the Delano table-grape strike ironically pitted many American-born children of immigrants against other American-born children of immigrants. The strikers' leader, César Chávez, was born an American in Arizona's Gila Valley.

He was the third generation to live on his grandfather's hundred-acre ranch before unpaid taxes and the Depression left him and his family homeless migrants in a 1927 Studebaker. "Some had been born into the migrant stream," he said. "But we had been on the land, and I knew a different life."

The two biggest vineyard owners in Delano at the time of the strike were what my dad used to call "bedroom farmers"—in this case, Schenley Industries and the DiGiorgio Corporation—absentee owners whose farms were a fraction of their corporate interests. Many of the other thirty-six Delano farmers were the children of immigrants—Italians, Armenians, and Croatians—not that far from migration and poverty themselves.

Delano was a hundred miles away from Rose, but she responded to the strike emotionally as an accusation of moral wrongdoing by farmers. At the time nearly four-fifths of Chicanos and Mexicans in the state lived in cities and towns, mostly in barrios, where many faced discrimination in jobs, housing, and schools. City liberals, though, pointed fingers at ranchers and farmers. "What particularly infuriated Delano ranchers," John Gregory Dunne wrote in an early book about the strike, "was the clergy's insistence that the situation involved not simply a labor issue but a moral issue." It was the movement, not the union, casting judgment on their way of life as a moral failing that enraged the ranchers.

Although the strike didn't affect Madera County because it wasn't big table-grape country, my dad as a valley rancher jumped into the fray and wrote a pamphlet titled *Delano: Another Crisis for the Catholic Church*, which as far as I was concerned at the time embarrassingly missed the point as much as did the cries about Chávez's Trotsky flag and a Bolshevik conspiracy. When the Catholic bishops sided with the farmworkers against the growers, gloom settled over many Catholic valley homes. A leading Delano farmer, Martin Zaninovich, the son of Croatian immigrants and the uncle of my high school classmate Marko Zaninovich, called for growers to cut off money to the Church.

During the ongoing activities of the United Farm Workers of America, Rose left the Catholic Church. A decade after farmers had signed union contracts, she said, "César Chávez has made great strides and has done great things for his people and for the farmworker," but "he has gone too far," particularly when, in Rose's view, he initiated a statewide ballot proposition that would invade growers' property rights and become "the beginning of an invasion of civil and constitutional rights of every American throughout our nation. The California farmworkers are the highest paid and the best housed of any State in the Union."

"I was born in the Catholic Church," Rose wrote, but the "deep church involvement in the farm movements drew me away from the Catholic Church. I am now a born-again Christian and attend the Believers Church."

I don't recall Rose speaking about God so much as about individual dignity and freedom. "The world is run by second-rate people," she later wrote. "The best are speedily crucified, or else never heard of until long after they are dead." After death, the "mark that man leaves behind is the imprint of the life he has lived through the morals he's practiced." That's why "man's sincere desire to progress morally is the awakening of his conscience to keep separate right from wrong."

The man in Rose's life after Nat's death was Ferd Beatty, a farmer who spent a lot of time behind the bar pouring drinks. We could flop dice with Ferd, notably Liar's Dice for drinks, double or nothing. By this time Rose owned a big chunk of Ripperdan Corner, listed in county records as the tavern she operated and the businesses she leased, including a grocery store, a welding shop, and an auto repair garage. Rose's house remained in the back lot, but Ferd didn't stay there. Rose provided him with his own little cabin behind the bar. There was no hypocrisy in this arrangement; it was open and unquestioned. All I knew was that Rose had some kind of relationship with Ferd. More than that was none of my business.

Short Watson, who knew his fellow rancher Ferd well and hunted with him, told me, "Ferd had his own place on a forty-acre vineyard. He usually stayed in the little house behind the bar when he got too drunk to go home."

Ferd had been in Rose's life for some time when an insurance salesman named Mack Brock showed up. "The guy cut Ferd out," Short said. "Rose fell head over heels for the guy. I couldn't understand it. She was crazy about him."

Brock was six years younger than Rose, six feet tall and 165 pounds. Born in Tennessee, he'd served as a warrant officer and first lieutenant in the Second World War. He'd had two years of college. When he enlisted, he was married to Rita C. Brock in Chattanooga. In 1945 he married Pearl Cheely from Oklahoma. After the war he married Leone McGinty from Missouri, making him now a possible trigamist, and settled in California, where he worked in Covina, Richmond, Stockton, and Oakland for thirteen years before coming alone to Madera.

When Mack moved into Rose's life, Ferd moved out. "I guess he long-cocked old Ferd," Short said. Mack was now the man behind the bar pouring drinks.

Two years later, on Monday, August 26, 1963, the Sheriff's Department got a call around midnight that Mack Brock had shot himself in a house behind the Farmer's Roundup. He was forty-six.

I asked Short, "What happened out there?"

"Rose shot him," Short said. "That's what everyone said. She said he committed suicide. I don't believe she really shot him, but a lot of guys did. There was hell of a talk around town, I'll tell you that. Ferd's uncle called her the Black Widow."

The day after the shooting, on Tuesday, August 27, 1963, *The Madera Tribune* reported on the front page that a "Ripperdan area man, apparently despondent over ill health, died shortly before midnight Monday from a self-inflicted bullet wound."

The dead man's name was misspelled in the paper as "Mack L. Breck, 46, a bartender at the Farmer's Roundup in the Ripperdan district."

According to investigating sheriff's officers, late Monday night Mack had "phoned his employer Mrs. Marchetti and told her he intended to take his life." As Rose approached the house where Mack lived behind the bar "she heard a shot and found Breck slumped over on the edge of his bed." The article concluded: "Death is believed by authorities to have been caused from a single bullet from a 38 cal. revolver found near the body. Body was removed to Jay's Chapel where services are pending."

There were no services, no autopsy, no obituary, no inquest, and no subsequent newspaper articles in the valley. The body was shipped north to an Oakland mortuary and buried in Golden Gate National Cemetery, the nearest veterans' cemetery, 170 miles from Madera. I later discovered that Mack came from a distinguished Tennessee family. His real name was Mack L. Brock, Jr. His third wife, Leone, was living in Alameda at the time, but it was Mack's cousin, William Emerson Brock, Jr., president of the Brock Candy Company of Chattanooga, who paid for the body's shipment and burial. Mack's father had been the firm's vice president until his death. Mack's uncle, William Emerson Brock, Sr., had founded the company and served as a U.S. senator. After Mack's death, another cousin, William Emerson Brock III, served in both the house and senate and as U.S. secretary of labor for Ronald Reagan.

The mortuary in Oakland recorded Brock's occupation as a bartender in "JAP Corners" in Madera but said nothing about the cause of his death.

Some fifty years later, in 2014, when I read *The Madera Tribune*'s account of Brock's death to Short Watson, he said, "That's completely Rose's story, right?" I said it was. "That's what makes it hard to figure out," Short said, "whether he really did it or she did. That's what makes it interesting as hell. She had a good story. Was it Rose's pistol?"

"Nobody knows," I told him. "I couldn't find anything here in town. Jay's Chapel had no record because it was a coroner's case. I finally located a county death certificate saying suicide, but it wasn't signed by the Madera coroner. The Sheriff's Department told me they couldn't find anything in their files, no investigative report, no coroner's report, nothing."

Short, who was then ninety-three, said, "They didn't do much investigating. About fifty percent of the people think she did it. So many stories took off from that, it's hard to tell. I didn't think she did myself, but she may have. Because you get to thinking back and she really fell for the old boy. She kicked Ferd's ass out and took him in."

After Mack's death, things returned to normal at Rose's with Ferd again behind the bar, pouring drinks, and Rose defending the farmer and the American Way.

At the end of the summer, three years later, we had a going-away barbecue on my family's ranch before I headed across country to graduate school. Rose came with lasagna she'd cooked for the occasion. After homemade ice cream we all danced to records in the barn. I danced with Rose.

A few months later, when my father was being touted in valley newspapers for a state appointment as secretary of agriculture, my friend Jim Unti sent me a letter back east. "I see that your father is giving up on these quasi-political organizations," Jim wrote, "and is going to get right to the top of things. Maybe he should get Rose to take his case to the governor-elect. If Reagan turns Rose down—well, that's just plain un-American."

Four years later Governor Reagan appointed Rose to the Madera County Fair Board, and as chair of the board she introduced the governor at the fall's agricultural festivities.

Just before turning eighty, Rose rode through town on a float as the Grand Marshal of the Old Timers Day Parade.

At a big party for her eightieth birthday, she gave a speech. "After this party was confirmed," she told partygoers, "at night, after I went to bed I would let my mind drift back as far as I could remember, and this is what I came up with. I will ask all of you to take a walk with me over my road of life. In all of this, there was its heartache and its humor."

Her reminiscences ran the gamut from her birth on the Fourth of July and her ranch-girl childhood to the current teaching of sex in schools, the widespread use of drugs, gays coming out of their closets, and marriage going out of style.

A year later, when she was eighty-one, she sold her bar and other property in Ripperdan Corner.

She'd already moved into town, and Ferd lived in the little house she built for him behind hers. Her address was 309 North E Street. His was 309½ North E Street.

About Mack Brock, the salesman who died in her house of a pistol shot, Rose later told Short Watson, "I don't know why I ever fell for that guy."

Chief Kit Fox Revisited

"I wish I could see you," Richard Palacioz told me. At our grammar school reunion he wore wraparound dark glasses and leaned on a cane. Five years earlier he'd had a stroke and lost all his peripheral eyesight. Then he had a heart attack. "It was caused by Agent Orange," he said. A little vision remained. "It's like looking through two straws."

A year later, when I visited him at his home in Madera, he was no longer able to get around with just a cane and had to use a walker. "His balance is really bad," his wife, Teri, said. His vision had closed to pinholes. "It's getting worse," Richard said. "He can't remember short-term," Teri added.

Next to me on his couch, with dark hair and a bushy mustache, seventy-five-year-old Richard looked shrunken with thinner legs than the previous year, but he still had the big smile and vigorous laugh I remembered from elementary school.

He laughed intermittently as he told Teri about the fake-wrestling matches we used to perform as kids. "We slugged each other but it wouldn't hurt," he told her. "We made it sound like we were hitting each other. Everything was planned right down to the last punch, the last flip."

Richard, now blind and immobile on his couch, was the most athletic of us grammar school grapplers back in those days when we writhed in phony pain from faked blows to the jaw and kicks to the head in imitation of the pro wrestlers we'd seen at the Veterans Memorial Auditorium in Fresno. At our grammar school reunion, some of us huddled over my laptop to look at the shaky home movie my father had taken of us practicing our routine on our ranch house lawn. Although he couldn't see himself in those blurry images, it was Richard, as Chief Kit Fox in war paint, who flew highest, leaped, and flung both feet up in pro-style dropkicks. It was Richard, as the wild Indian, who bounced most dramatically after I flipped him through the air or turned him upside down and body-slammed him to the ground.

And this was just an unpolished practice. "We weren't at our best," as I always complained about the film. What still comes through in the silence of this grainy movie is the genuineness of Richard's smile before and after our wild mêlée on the grass. His grin returned across the years as the beacon of his good-natured disposition, something I could expect to encounter with constancy in the schoolyard. We all appeared happy in the movie. Richard looked joyful.

"We wanted to put on a demonstration at the Harvest Festival," Richard told Teri. We were practicing our wrestling performance one night in the outdoor ring set up for real boxing matches during the festival. The former pro boxer who'd arranged the bouts climbed into the ring to break us up. "He stopped us," Richard said, laughing, "because he thought we were actually killing each other."

In high school, Richard went on to join the real wrestling team and to play football. "My two cousins Frank and Ace Rodriguez were state wrestling champions," he said, "and I wanted to follow behind them. When my knees got infected from mat burns they wouldn't allow me to wrestle anymore."

His knees didn't bother the Marine Corps when he enlisted after graduation from high school. Following boot camp in San Diego, he was transferred to Camp Lejeune in North Carolina, where, he said, "They nicknamed me Pancho." The reason for the name made sense to him. "It was because I was the only Mexican in the whole company." There were maybe ten or eleven other Hispanics, but they were all Puerto Ricans. "Everybody knew me as Pancho." The majority of Marines there were from the South. "I got along with them fine. In fact, one of my best buddies was from Alabama—A. G. Cook. He was a good friend of mine." Richard has stayed in touch with him. He asked Teri, "We still have his address, don't we, dear?"

After four years in the Marines, Richard reenlisted and became a drill instructor, a military role of such feigned sadism that I had a hard time seeing this sweet-natured and slight-statured vet enacting it. "When I went through training," Richard said, "my drill instructor beat the heck out of us. He'd stand us up right there in the front door of his hooch and ask us questions. When we got them wrong, he hit us right in the stomach. We'd straighten up and he'd hit us again."

I told Richard that I had two nephews—one in the navy and one in the army—who'd served a total of three tours in Iraq, and I'd had the chance to see a drill sergeant, the term of designation and address for training instructors in the army, at work after my nephew Caleb's graduation from boot camp in Fort Jackson, South Carolina. During the afternoon, I stood with my brother and his family in the VIP tent during graduation because Caleb had earned the award during basic training for the company's highest PT scores. A drill sergeant told my brother how outstanding his son was. "We don't see anyone like him except, maybe, every three or four cycles," the drill sergeant said.

That night, though, my nephew was just another soldier lined up at attention in front of the barracks as a drill sergeant screamed and shouted, saying they were the worst group of maggots he'd ever encountered and he wasn't going to reenlist because of them. He'd just gotten word of another friend killed in Iraq and he was damned mad. I watched from a distance, hidden in shadows. With each of his insults and orders, the men and women who'd graduated that day shouted back, "Yes, Drill Sergeant."

"You worms disgust me," he shouted.

"Yes, Drill Sergeant."

"Your mommy and daddy and boyfriend and girlfriend were just here. Now they're gone. They don't exist. Do you understand?"

"Yes, Drill Sergeant."

"I exist."

"Yes, Drill Sergeant."

"And your job is to make me happy."

"Yes, Drill Sergeant."

"And you are going to clean your barracks until you make me real happy."

And on and on. I turned to Richard and asked, "Were you like that?"

He laughed and said, "Yeah. In fact, I had one kid raising and holding an artillery shell over his head and he kept dropping it. I told him, 'You drop it one more time and I'm going to bust your jaw.' He dropped it and I hit him and broke his jaw. After his mouth started bleeding, I said, 'Oh my God.' I forgot he already had a broken jaw and had barely healed. He was cut back a couple of months, and we'd just picked him up to train him. I said, 'Well, that's it for my career,' but he never said I hit him."

Teri joked, "All my cousins call him Sarge. He tries to pull the DI on me but it doesn't stick."

"I was a drill instructor for two years," Richard said, "then I got my orders for Vietnam." In Vietnam, he said, "We had blacks, Hispanics, every nationality." Richard was the platoon sergeant, second in command. "We were understaffed. We only had eighteen, we were supposed to have thirty-seven." They went on search-and-destroy and ambush missions designed for a full platoon. They carried M16 rifles. "I never liked that rifle," Richard said, "because it would jam all the time. You get a little dust in it and it would jam. I'd rather have the M14. You could bury it in the ground and it would still fire.

"We would go out as soon as it got dark and set up night ambushes. We didn't even know if we were in the right area. Whoever walked into the ambush got killed. There was one night I'll always remember."

Through the distant trees he saw a little light that kept flashing on and off like a lightning bug. "I called one of my squad leaders over and said, 'Look at that. Do you see that light flashing on and off?'"

The squad leader replied, "That's probably a lightning bug."

"They don't have lightning bugs in Vietnam," Richard told him.

He lay on the ground next to a tree for a few minutes and watched the light flash on and off. "I put my rifle on fully automatic and let out a whole burst. You could see the little light start bouncing off the branches. It was a flashlight from some Vietcong or NVA." The platoon had to return to its station before daybreak. "We took off before it got light and I didn't even go back to see who it was. I'll always remember that. Once that little light started bouncing off the tree branches I knew I hit him." Richard paused. "I hardly ever really talk about Vietnam."

He was in Quàng Tri Province in 1968. "That's where I was mostly," he said, a region heavily sprayed with Agent Orange. "It was supposed to be a defoliant. I'd hate to be the Vietnamese they sprayed it on—probably none of them are living. Without letting those people know they just sprayed the whole Quàng Tri Province."

I told him about my cousin, who was a Marine killed in adjoining Quàng Nam Province, another Agent Orange hot spot in the Da Nang cluster.

"When was that?"

"The year after you were there, 1969."

"That was a bad time in Vietnam," Richard said. "Well, they were all bad."

After a year in Vietnam he returned to San Diego, where he received redeployment orders for another combat tour. "All my buddies," he said, "that had been to Nam and never got a scratch, when they got their orders to go back they got their legs blown off and killed and everything else, so I said, 'This is it for me,' but when I got to Okinawa they told me, 'No, you've been there. You don't have to go back again.'"

He'd put ten years into the Marines and was getting ready to enlist a third time. "I would've stayed and made a career of it, but my first wife told me if you reenlist I'll divorce you. It was the Marine Corps or my wife, so I got out. I should've stayed in because I was divorced eight years later anyway. Except for Vietnam, I really enjoyed the Marines."

He applied to be a corrections officer in California but was rejected. "I put down that I'd been a brig guard at the naval station for two years after Vietnam, and I think because of that they didn't allow me to become a corrections officer." Teri disagreed, saying that her brother had been in corrections and if applicants had any previous training as guards in a boys' club or elsewhere they'd be accepted.

"They didn't accept me," Richard said. "They didn't give a reason. They just said I wasn't accepted."

"Did you take a test?" Teri asked.

Richard said he'd taken the test in Fresno. "I got 97 percent."

"That's weird," Teri said.

Richard worked for fourteen years as a carpenter and cement finisher for a local construction company and then moved to the olive-canning plant as the only carpenter in the facility. He learned how to fly C-150s, those little puddle jumpers, just for fun. During this time he met and married Teri. He liked working in construction. "The plant supervisor told everyone not to mess with me or tell me what to do." His brother Reggie, who was also with us in grammar school, ended up in Washington, where his wife's family had followed the harvests, picking cherries and other crops, until Reggie became a barber. "But he calls himself a hair stylist," Richard said. He and his brother had both escaped life as farmworkers.

"They retired me at sixty," Richard said. Three years later the blood vessels at the back of his brain ruptured. He lost his sight, was able to see only shadows, and spent six months at the VA hospital in Palo Alto, learning how to feed himself and to walk alone in a residential area and listen for cars when about to cross streets with a walker. Teri went up for her own training and wore goggles with pinholes to understand what he was going through.

Two months after returning home from the hospital in 2007 he had a heart attack. Three years later, in 2010, he received a letter saying that one of the side effects of Agent Orange was a heart attack. Since he'd been exposed to the chemical and had a heart attack, he was eligible for compensation.

I asked if Agent Orange also caused the stroke. "They didn't specify anything else," Richard said. Before his stroke he'd been receiving a hundred dollars a month from the Veterans Administration because he'd tested positive for post-traumatic stress disorder.

"He would go through some things," Teri said, "like, wow, I couldn't understand it. He would never tell me. He would go off and hide and get drunk, and I said what is going on with you?"

When I asked Richard what kinds of things he thought about, he replied, "I would think about my buddy Frank, he got killed, and Donald got wounded, the guys in the service…" His voice trailed off, then picked up. "I always had flashbacks from the time I got out of the Marine Corps. My ex-wife woke up just in time once when I was swinging and hit her pillow where her head was." She was his second wife. "I would be fighting in my sleep."

"He still does that," Teri said. They've now been married fourteen years, longer than both of his previous wives put together, the third time, she says, being a charm. "He moves a lot, kicks, and talks in his sleep."

Richard will occasionally have a cigarette and a drink but very seldom. He quit both after his stroke. "His drinking really stopped then," Teri said.

"And when did it really start?" I asked Richard. "When you got out of the Marines?"

"No, I was drinking in the Marine Corps. We had the enlisted men's club, and anyone in the service could go there and drink beer."

"One thing I have to say about Richard," Teri said, "is since all this happened to him he's never questioned why—why me?—why did this happen to me?"

"I never blamed anybody for it," Richard said.

"He only had himself to blame," Teri said.

I interrupted, thinking about the codes of manhood and toughness in the valley we grew up with, all those restrictions on complainers who blame others for their plight. I asked him, "You can't blame yourself for Agent Orange, can you?"

"Well," he said, "my heart attack was caused by Agent Orange."

"But the stroke was from the smoking and the drinking," Teri said.

"Yeah," Richard said, "and that's when I quit."

Reading Didion

I'm a longtime admirer of Joan Didion. I recall my excitement in my twenties when reading her essays in *Slouching Towards Bethlehem* to discover the little town of Madera, where I grew up, aptly linked to Didion's own hometown of Sacramento and other California valley towns, connected through the implacable insularity of their nineteenth-century frontier way of thinking. Didion swam in the Sacramento River, while I swam in the San Joaquin, but I recognized the intense August heat she evoked so well as an affliction, the flat valley ranches, the winter tule fog, the rising rivers, the broken levees, and the floods. Some forty years later in *Where I Was From*, Didion wrote about the painful loss of her romantic visions of California. She claimed she now could confront "only obliquely" her "confusions" about the place and the way she grew up. She's right about her confusions, for a troubling absence marks four decades of her otherwise illuminating writing about her valley experience and California's history. The great blind spot of her work is that she doesn't see beyond stereotypes the Dust Bowl refugees she went to school with or recognize the many ways the original Okies and their sons and daughters altered the valley and the state.

In *Where I Was From* Didion tells us how her revisionist thoughts about California arose, in part, when she realized at a late date that certain aspects of her eighth-grade graduation speech, titled "Our California Heritage," "did not add up" because she had delivered it to an audience of children and parents who had for the most part arrived in California during the 1930s, refugees from the Dust Bowl. Her implication is that the Dust Bowl migrant experience and her own California heritage were worlds apart and she'd left their experience out of her childhood speech. Didion at this point says nothing about these Okie refugees or their great impact on the valley and the state. She says nothing about the difference between her upbringing and theirs. Instead, she slides away from the topic to launch into a disquisition about government-subsidized dam building and irrigation projects in the Great Central Valley.

Omissions often produce what's most engaging about Didion's cool, portentous style. To sidestep painful facts and raw emotions surrounding the deaths of a husband and daughter as she does in other books is understandable. Less explicable is the avoidance of social changes Didion says she's going to talk about in relation to Dust Bowl migrants and then doesn't. I'm not alone in feeling frustrated with such elusiveness. Novelist and essayist Meghan Daum, author of *The Problem with Everything: My Journey Through the New Culture Wars*, wrote in a review, "I often found myself exasperated by Didion's relentless opacity...I wanted some straighter talk....But to read Didon, especially over the last decade, is often to feel awash in unanswered questions."

In *Where I Was From*, when Didion examines the enormous changes migration has brought to California, she gives the percentages of population growth for each decade immediately after statehood, from 1850 to 1880. For the twentieth-century population boom, she cites the increases in the decades from the early years of immigration to the onset of the Depression—1900–10, 1910–20, 1920–30—and the post-war increases for 1940–50 and 1950–60. About the big migration of 1930–40, Didion gives no statistics. Inexplicably she says nothing about the major decade of Dust Bowl refugees.

The historian James N. Gregory, in *American Exodus: The Dust Bowl Migration and Okie Culture in California* (1989), describes the exodus between 1910 and 1930 when close to one and a half million migrants, mainly from Oklahoma, Texas, Arkansas, and Missouri, left their home states, with a quarter of them settling in California as generic "Okies," while others migrating northward were simply labeled "hillbillies." Nearly another half-million Dust Bowl refugees arrived in California in 1930–40 to raise the number of these newcomers to eleven percent of the state's population. By 1950, Okies constituted thirteen percent of California's population and twenty-two percent of the San Joaquin Valley—statistics, it would seem, noteworthy for Didion's book about California and its Great Valley.

The word *Okie* doesn't appear in Didion's *Where I Was From*. It is mentioned in *Slouching Towards Bethlehem*, when she notes how the word *downtown* in the Great Valley is "pronounced *down*town with the Okie accent that now pervades Valley speech patterns." This sociological indication of Okie culture's influence throughout the valley became personal when Didion told a *New York Times* reporter that the almost Southern softness in her voice is, in her words, "an Okie accent picked up in Sacramento high schools." Who are these Okies? In *Slouching Towards Bethlehem*, Didion identifies them as "the flotsam of the new California." In *The White Album*, she labels them as part of the "stuff of bad dreams" haunting her—"all the ignorant armies jostling in the night"—including those of "children burning in the locked car in the supermarket parking lot...the hustlers, the insane, the cunning Okie faces that turn up in military investigations, the sullen lurking in doorways."

This much-quoted selection, highlighted in the introduction to Didion's *Collected Nonfiction* in 2006, would seem unimaginable had she labeled "the hustlers, the insane, the cunning Okie faces" as Jewish or Black or Asian or Mexican. Although Okie pride and redneck chic became socially acceptable in the valley, even fashionable in the wake of the new ethnic consciousness of the 1960s and 1970s, those Okie faces belong to part of the last ethnic group of Americans in the West and Southwest that it's still okay to vilify or lampoon.

Gerald Haslam, the percipient California writer and author of the story collection *Okies*, described Didion as "the gifted writer who seems to be the East's California expert" and "appears to be ignorant of and unsympathetic toward the vast working and middle classes." Didion does show concern in her writings for the underclass in New York City, where she lives, but this same awareness doesn't extend across the country to where she was from. The point for both Haslam and me is not to accuse Didion of distinctive Okie discrimination but to identify a widespread, unthinking, class-bound prejudice shared with many Americans, whether politically conservative or liberal. A valley friend of mine, now an Ivy League professor, told me he sees a lot of his own inclinations and biases in Didion, what he calls "my own discomfort with working-class whites of the Central Valley." He adds how the conflict between poor whites and poor non-whites might also be reflected in Didion. "It's easier to explain crime or poverty if someone is of another race (and thus either inferior or subject to discrimination, depending on your social views)."

Unrestricted to Didion or to California, ongoing slurs in the broader American culture toward certain groups of struggling whites go unnoticed and encompass social class rather than simply region, as Senator Jim Webb indicates in his objection to Hollywood's safe ridiculing of poor Southern whites as stereotypical "rednecks," a term he finds offensive. In his public comments and writings, particularly in *Born Fighting: How the Scots-Irish Shaped America*, Webb has been leading the way in a

largely unsuccessful effort to make Americans recognize a prev-
alent though largely unacknowledged class-bound prejudice
against an entire group of Old Appalachian and mainly Ulster-
Scots descendants. These Americans of Ulster-Scots heritage
include the Okies John Steinbeck wrote about: Californians
and their descendants who according to Didion are newcomers
of vague lineage but whose ties to the American soil ironically
go back to colonial times, as do hers, though sometimes longer
than hers since many are also of mixed Choctaw or Cherokee or
Muscogee or other Native American heritage.

In her attempt to sort out her revised thoughts about California, and particularly the Great Valley, Didion seeks aid from
earlier writers but not from John Steinbeck, who wrote the only
novel about the 1930s California Okie migration to be published
in the twentieth century. In 1939, the New York editor Bennett
Cerf had planned to publish an "exceptionally fine" valley novel,
Whose Names Are Unknown, by the Oklahoma writer Sanora Babb,
but after the appearance of *The Grapes of Wrath* he changed his
mind. "Obviously," he wrote to Babb, "another book at this
time about exactly the same subject would be a sad anticlimax."
Babb's novel was eventually published in 2004 by the University
of Oklahoma Press.

In *Where I Was From*, Didion quotes the California writings of
the philosopher Josiah Royce and the political economist Henry
George, the nature essays of John Muir, the ranch memoirs of
Jane Hollister Wheelwright, and the poetry of Robinson Jeffers,
all focusing on California. She provides an extensive analysis
of two important California novels, Frank Norris's *The Octopus*
and Jack London's *The Valley of the Moon*, and she even looks
closely at William Faulkner's atypical California short story,
"Golden Land," but she doesn't mention *The Grapes of Wrath* or
In Dubious Battle or any of Steinbeck's novels or stories or the

Okies in them. On the occasion of the centennial of Steinbeck's birth, I happened to be one of forty-six writers, ranging from Norman Mailer to Harper Lee, to offer brief remarks, sometimes no more than a couple of sentences, in *John Steinbeck: Centennial Reflections by American Writers*. Didion declined to contribute.

What's going on here? Didion has no obligation to like Steinbeck's work. Many readers of Dust Bowl heritage find his portraits of Okies demeaning. But to mention every major California writer except him seems odd. I'm sometimes asked what psychological factors might have influenced Didion's silence toward Okies. Did something happen in her past with her classmates to compel her to suppress that side of her California background? There's no need to speculate about such possible psychological events. The formation of her social class bias isn't elusive. As a fifth-generation Californian, she recalls running with a dog over the same flat fields her great-great-grandfather had found virgin and had planted in "the real Valley." Westerners on both sides of her pioneering family crossed the Great Plains by wagon in the middle of the nineteenth century, a crossing, she says, able to render her miserable and guilty when she makes her own transcontinental crossings by jet. As I mentioned, my paternal Béarnais great-grandparents made a different western crossing by boat and train from the French Pyrenees to California in the 1870s. Later, my maternal Basque grandparents made similar crossings from Bizkaia to Nevada in 1897 and 1910. Unlike my immigrant family, Didion says her family has "always" been in California.

For those of us who grew up in the valley, Didion's formative years make her early class bias understandable, something almost no one in her position could avoid. Her longtime friend and advocate, John Leonard, the former editor of *The New York Times Book Review*, wrote that since the middle of the nineteenth century Didion's family "lived in California with a ranchero sense of entitlement." She grew up in dark houses, wore clothes of muted Pre-Raphaelite colors, and draped her shoulders with her great-grandmother's black lace mantilla for school dances. She learned to favor old, greenish copper and tarnished silver. She grew up with the idea she acknowledges as romantic that California had been spoiled. Change meant decline, such as someone's choice, she says, to vacation on Maui rather than to take the cruise ship *Lurline* to the traditional Hawaiian destination of Honolulu. Another sign of decline was someone's choosing to go back east to college at Princeton rather than the traditional choice of Berkeley or Stanford. Even bigger decline occurred with the breakup of big ranches into subdivisions with names like Rancho Del Rio No. 1 and Rancho Del Rio No. 3, filling with the descendants of "new people" her grandfather vilified.

"All that is constant about the California of my childhood," Didion writes in *Slouching Towards Bethlehem*, "is the rate at which it disappears." Old ranches go under and sleepy valley towns with frame houses dwindle as the "new people" move in. Her first novel, *Run River*, published in 1963, spews out a litany of negative responses to cheaply dressed Wops, cheating Mexicans, and dumb Okies with an effectively aware dramatization of social prejudice in the 1940s and 1950s that many of us shared and now look back on with embarrassment. Like Didion and the characters in *Run River*, I grew up in the valley when widespread use of the term *Okie* ranged from the neutrally descriptive to the derogatory. At my father's breakfast table, I heard his ranch foreman, a self-defined Okie, describe how the previous night in a bar fight the foreman's brothers had "knocked some redneck Okies from pillar to post," phrasing that clearly distinguished himself and his brothers on the social ladder. A memorable climactic moment in *Run River* occurs when a young man calls his girlfriend of old California stock "Okie bitch," meaning that like other Okie girls we see in the novel she's a slut. This young man is himself from Tennessee but mistakenly identified by the girl's father as from Mississippi. When corrected, the old California landowner lumps the boyfriend in with other California flotsam, both white and black. "Mississippi, Tennessee, what's the difference...It's all Del Paso Heights to me." Del Paso Heights, we're told, is "a district north of Sacramento noted for its large Negro population and its high incidence of minor social disorders."

What's puzzling is Didion's silence about these class-bound attitudes in the reconsideration of her childhood in *Where I Was From*. She chides her overheated first novel, *Run River*, for its nostalgic romanticism but doesn't examine the dark side of her upbringing and its social-class prejudices and slurs. She swings from one extreme of nostalgia to another in exchanging her view as a melancholy romantic for one as a weary, disappointed Westerner. She comes to recognize an unflattering continuity between Old and New California: it was always a place where those entering the state, including her own family, took what they could and sold off the rest to get rich, leaving California in hock to corporate America and the government. "True" Californians hadn't resisted change, they welcomed it. Millions of acres of farmland sold off and developed after the breakup of giant ranches like Miller & Lux, Irvine, and Hollister help Didion to revise her earlier romantic views of California settlement. The myth of self-reliant pioneering settlers in the Great Valley gets scrapped in her work for a new image of agribusiness—big capitalist enterprises run by absentee owners and entrepreneurs dependent on federal subsidies. Almost no one in California, Didion claims, speaks of "farmers" in the normal sense of the word. Her new myth of a totally corporate agribusiness in California disregards all of the valley's farming families of immigrant stock. Didion's fascination with huge ranches also disregards the people who worked on them. She replaces a commonplace myth about legendary individualistic pioneers with another about faceless greedy corporations.

Didion's replacement of one commonplace myth with another demonstrates her inability to understand why her differing views of California pioneers and Dust Bowl children "did not add up." She offers this explanation: "Not much about California, on its own preferred terms, has encouraged its children to see themselves as connected to one another." She doesn't connect the Dust Bowl history of the parents and children she addressed at her eighth-grade graduation with the "Defense Okies" in Aerojet factories during the Second World War or the McDonnell Douglas aerospace workers she writes about in Lakewood in the 1990s. In *Where I Was From*, she remains silent about the children who apparently influenced the lifelong intonations of her speech. She doesn't connect the dots. In an earlier essay, however, excerpted in both *The White Album* and her *Collected Nonfiction*, Didion most fully registers her sense of the California children of the Dust Bowl.

"Nine Bike Movies in Seven *Vroom!* Days," originally published in *Life* in May 1970, is in many ways technically brilliant, a model of how to structure an essay. Didion defines the spate of cheaply made biker movies of the time, like *The Wild Angels* and *Hell's Angels on Wheels* and *The Glory Stompers*, always set in the West, as forming a kind of underground folk literature for adolescents "to express that audience's every inchoate resentment." Adults, she says, rarely see these films, known as "programmers." To see nine biker films in one week, some on double and triple bills, Didion drove out of Los Angeles to drive-ins and theaters in Tarzana and as far as Bakersfield in the San Joaquin Valley, near the setting of *The Grapes of Wrath*, though she doesn't say so.

In a theater Didion overhears a girl of fourteen or fifteen tell her mother how the motorcycle gang on the screen let an innocent driver off easy after the bikers forced his car off the road, shot out his tires, ripped open his hood, and smashed what seemed to be the carburetor's air filter over his head. The unprovoked violence of these movies, Didion says, reflects the resentment and irritability of the young moviegoers she encountered, "the extent to which a nonexistent frustration threshold is seen not as psychopathic but as a 'right.'" Biker chicks acting dumb deservedly get turned out for the gang. A waitress not providing instant service also gets gang-banged, the restaurant torn apart, and the owner left for dead. "Rev up the Harleys and ride." A successful biker movie, Didion maintains, provides a perfect Rorschach of its audience, and with uncharacteristic directness she identifies the adolescent audience of these films in an astonishing sentence:

> To imagine the audience for whom these sentiments
> are tailored, I suppose you need to have sat in a lot of
> drive-ins yourself, to have gone to school with boys
> who majored in shop and worked in gas stations and
> later held them up, to know all those children of vague
> "hill" stock who grow up absurd in the West and South-
> west, children whose whole lives are an obscure grudge
> against a world they think they never made.

This accusatory generalization about "vague 'hill' stock" and "an obscure grudge against a world" stereotypes two generations of Okie children in terms of a criminal impulse, mongrel genealogy, and unjustified resentment, while remaining forgetful of how or why these kids really grew up—absurd or not—in a world of prejudice they encountered but certainly didn't make. There's nothing obscure about hungry eyes and reactionary bitterness in response to one class stepping on another. In *Where I Was From*, the conspicuous blank space in the middle of Didion's portrayal of the Great Central Valley helps explain why some forty years later California still loomed before her, on her own preferred terms, as "impenetrable" and "a wearying enigma." Her stance as a romantic Westerner in *Slouching Towards Bethlehem* and as a disappointed romantic in *Where I Was From* gives edge to her vignettes of a California in decline, but exchanging one set of myths for another sustains a blind spot and creates, in her phrasing, a "fable of confusion" about the details of social history and the realities of American social class keeping the children of California and the West—the children of America—disconnected.

Black Farm Kid and the Okies

As a farm boy, Theodore Marshall Payne grew up in a patch of Madera County called Dixieland, where his family of fourteen kids grew cotton after his parents moved to the San Joaquin Valley from Louisiana a few years before Ted was born. "We owned the property," he said. "We still do. As property owners, we got money from the gin to hire people to chop and weed cotton. These guys would come migrating through Dixieland in trailers and lowbeds with sleeping quarters on them—fieldworkers, whites, Okies." Ted recalls walking along the road with his brothers and friends to Dixieland Elementary School when the white field hands who might work for his family would pass and shout at them, "Hey, niggers." The itinerant fieldworkers were calling the property owners names.

"I got called all kinds of names," Ted said. "My dad told me, 'The only difference between you and them is the pigment of your skin. God loves you.'"

Ted Payne feels lucky to have followed his dad's advice when growing up on a farm. He attended the Mennonite Church until his late teens, when he moved to the Baptist Church because his father wanted him to be an usher. His dad had worked for the railroad in Louisiana and saw what happened to a lot of people rolling dice, and as a result Ted and his brothers weren't allowed to play cards or dominoes at home. That's why his brothers Virgil and Jerry got into chess.

An old box spring served as a backstop on the farm when the boys played baseball. "When we went into town for Little League and they threw to us it was like hitting a pumpkin," Ted said. Mr. April coached the Rotary team and drove out to meet Ted and other country boys for practices at the Dixieland school and to drive them into town for games. Ted's dad told Mr. April he didn't want his boys in the streets, but he was assured he had nothing to worry about. "It was about achievement, it was about winning," Ted said. "When we won, we got floats." Root beer floats at the Reed and Bell stand. "No way were we going to lose."

About Mr. April, Ted said, "Frank and Ray were blessed to have a dad like him. At the reunion, I told Frank how great his folks were, especially to minorities. I'd talk to his mom and dad, they were like a second family to me."

When Ted was seven he got up at six in the morning to feed the goats, and when he was twelve he woke at four-thirty to milk the cows. After profit losses in cotton, his family made money with their dairy and vegetables. The Young brothers would drive their trucks from town to buy vegetables for their markets. "We used cow manure," Ted said, "not fertilizer. They were getting organic stuff in those days before there were organic farms." His family had its own smokehouse and made salt pork. "When we killed a hog, we'd grind it for sausages."

Ted worked on the farm while going to classes. He belonged to a 4-H club and made money by raising and selling swine, lamb, and beef. "4-H developed a lot of country kids," he said. "You learned about animal life and plants. It was good training. We'd get a Bank of America loan to buy sheep at Ceres and beef at Noble's. We'd show in Chowchilla, L.A., and the S.F. Cow Palace." Every day Ted would work a five-hundred-pound yearling with a halter until it fattened for sale at nine hundred pounds.

A turning point came in his senior year. To earn additional money he lived with a white family while taking care of their kids and getting up at 3:00 a.m. before school to load trucks with milk from their dairy. He was often doing his homework at ten and eleven at night. He got tired of it and told his father, "I'm going to run away."

"Okay," his dad replied, "if you don't want to go to school, go work in the fields."

Not wanting to be a farmhand, he stayed in school. At Dixieland in the eighth grade he won the American Legion Award. At Madera High he was elected the Boys Athletic Association president. In high school he was a three-sport athlete in wrestling, football, and baseball. At first he was undersized for football as a 103-pound freshman but grew to be a 138-pound sophomore, a 150-pound junior, and then a 172-pound senior. At the varsity football banquet he received the best sportsmanship award. Photos of the event show him looking scholarly, wearing horn-rims, a sports coat, and a tie, with a squared white handkerchief peeking from his breast pocket. At the annual Madera High Punch Bowl, he was judged the outstanding boxer.

Ted went on to wrestle and play baseball at Reedley College. He signed a minor league contract with the Pittsburgh Pirates. I looked up his record with the Kingsport Pirates in the Appalachian League, where he was listed at five-nine and 170 pounds, an infielder who threw right and batted left. He came to bat twenty-one times with an average of .286 and a slugging percentage of .381. His season in the minors was short, ending when he turned twenty-one and was drafted into the army, where he said, "I ended up being a jock." He was All-Army baseball and for three years on the All-Army wrestling team. As a first sergeant he spent ten years in Germany and Italy. "My wife didn't want me killing anybody," he told me, "and wanted me to come back to the States." After earning a master's degree in psychological counseling at Ball State, he was reclassified for a military occupation specialty (MOS) and worked in drug and alcohol counseling for the Veterans Administration and in school systems for twenty-two years. "A lot of my family ended up in education," he said. His brother Jerry became a superintendent of schools.

Ted retired from the army active reserve at sixty and made his home in the Salinas Valley. He returns to the San Joaquin Valley to visit his daughter Jetaime, who moved back to the valley after graduating from Brown. Ted also checks on his Dixieland property, near where my brother lived when he was starting out as a farrier. "All that country has changed," Ted said. His Dixieland farm is now leased out as an almond orchard.

When he was growing up he loved to fish and to hunt quail, pheasants, ducks, and deer in the valley and hills. "We used to have a lot of grain land in the valley; everything is now almonds," he said. Gamebirds have diminished. Although he's had two hip replacements, a knee replacement, and stents in his heart, he continues to hunt on an Oregon ranch he bought along the Columbia River. He's now looking into selling the ranch but considers himself lucky to have owned it. "No matter your color, it's about the chances you get," he told me. "You have to see what you can get for your money and what you like to do. I've been a blessed guy."

Things didn't turn out equally lucky for his brother Virgil, an African American community activist, shot and killed by two sheriff's deputies in Humboldt County, where he worked for the forestry service. "There were lots of drugs in the mountains," Ted said, "lots of weed around the College of Redwoods. Word was out that my brother was on to law enforcement supporting the weed deals." Virgil filed depositions against deputies for police violence against Hoopa Valley Indians. "He had an Indian fiancée; her brother was a teacher at the college." Virgil had been monitoring payoffs from marijuana growers to deputies near the Hoopa Valley Reservation. He'd also discovered deputies receiving kickbacks from methamphetamine producers on the reservation.

Deputies stopped Virgil outside the reservation. "They pulled him over," Ted said. "They said he was acting funny and shot him at close range. He didn't get any medical attention."

This was California in 1982. More than a hundred people demonstrated in front of the Humboldt Courthouse. Editorials called for open hearings. The NAACP filed a civil rights suit. "Law enforcement in Humboldt has a persistent record of violating the civil rights of minority peoples and then covering its own act," an NAACP lawyer said. "The sheriff and his deputies will have to appear down in San Francisco to explain why they had to shoot an unarmed young black man three times at close range with a .357 Magnum and then kick him so many times in the face that every bone in it was smashed."

At the courthouse, a journalist read the names of some twenty people of color who "have died on or in the vicinity of the Hoopa Reservation during the past decade under questionable circumstances and often with little investigation by the authorities." Sheriff's deputies killed five unarmed men, including Virgil, during that period, and no grand jury returned an indictment against the officers.

"We tried to get a wrongful death suit against them," Ted said. "We had T-shirts made up, but nothing came of it. They were acquitted. One of the officers was later killed. It's sad. Virgil was getting ready to go to the San Luis School of Forestry."

I asked about his own experience with racism, starting with the name-calling when he and Virgil were kids. "Not in high school," he said. He got along with all his classmates, no matter their race. In fact, he said, "I had a Hispanic in my family. Uncle Joaquín taught me how to prune and trim trees. I spoke Spanish. I developed an understanding."

With white boys from families like those who'd called him names along the road in Dixieland, he developed friendships, as he did with the toughest of them, Billy Carter. "Billy didn't come from a wealthy family. He wasn't Italian or Portuguese or someone's son," Ted said, indicating the social-class status certain immigrant families had achieved in the valley. "Billy was an Okie kid. Nobody wanted to mess with him. In shop, he could jump up and kick over a fifty-gallon barrel full of stuff and land on his feet. To move a barrel so heavy you had to push it over and roll it, but he could give it a flying kick with both feet and not fall down. Afterward, he'd drop to his hands and chest on the floor and do forty, fifty, sixty fast push-ups. In shop, we'd laugh and joke around. He told me, 'You're tough for a little guy. You can beat anybody your size, and I can beat anybody my size.' So we shared that kind of bond."

Ted went on: "Billy was excellent at fixing cars. I had a '39 Chevy and we had it up on four wheels." Billy helped Ted take the engine apart, change the brake pads, wheels, and all the rest. "He could take off a rim and change a tire in a minute," Ted said. "He was a bright guy. He liked to work hard. If he'd had the desire he could've done whatever he wanted. He could've been a teacher. He had the mannerisms, but he wanted to make money. He wasn't a drunk or bully or a hothead, but you knew not to rub him the wrong way. Challenge his manhood and it was on."

Besides being the toughest kid in town, Billy had lots of girlfriends. Ted recalled that as a sophomore Billy, though the youngest employee, was made the night manager at Walt's Gas Station. He had a locker there and often went straight from the station to school without going home. "Billy could shuck 'n' jive," Ted said. "A lot of people knew him. He always had a couple or three girlfriends, married women who'd cook him food, buy him clothes, give him money. He didn't spend a lot of time at home. When my dad killed a beef he gave meat to Billy and said, 'Now don't be giving it to a woman.'"

As high school kids in those days, we were pretty sure in our own narrow way that Madera had the toughest guys and the best-looking women in the valley. For evidence, there was Billy, who in fistfighting dominated the county from the valley floor to the mountains. In wrestling, Madera High regularly had champions. One year Madera wrestlers won five of twelve Northern California State Championships. You don't get much tougher than that.

As for girls, you only had to look in the yearbook. Guys from my boarding school were eager to hitchhike with me on weekends to Madera dances and parties. I know that's not hard evidence, but we enjoyed our blinkered view of the universe. A friend from those years, Jerry Weinberger, recently told me to check out some amusing outside confirmation in Jack Kerouac's *On the Road*. Kerouac and some friends pulled off Highway 99 at the edge of a San Joaquin Valley town. They sat in the car "digging the girls" in Mextown while eating a watermelon. "And then, as purple dusk descended over the grape country, I found myself sitting dumbly in the car," Kerouac writes. "All kinds of pretty little girls were cutting down the darkening street. I said, 'Where the hell are we?'" They were in Madera.

As an Okie kid, Billy exhibited the "cult of toughness" as James Gregory defined it in *American Exodus: The Dust Bowl Migration and Okie Culture*: persistence whether in street fights or at work; "there could be no dignity, manhood, or self-respect without it." Work was the flip side of fighting; both reflected toughness, a badge of honor shared with other working minorities in the valley. Oscar Zeta Acosta in *Autobiography of a Brown Buffalo* writes that for Chicano kids, "It seemed the sole purpose of childhood was to train boys how to be men. We had to get up early, run home from school, work on weekends, holidays and during vacations, all for the purpose of being men." Being a man, *un hombre*, also meant a willingness to fight. Acosta, who had several Okie buddies, said, "Okies were just as tough as the Mexicans." His father had taught him how to fight. "At night and on weekends we fought the Mexicans in the neighborhood, but during the day and at school we had to fight off the Okies."

Sometimes toughness and girls intertwined. Ted recalled a fight Billy had after a football game against the Merced Bears in their senior year. Word was out that Kenny Shelton, who'd graduated three or four years earlier and was in the Marines, was back in town because Billy had been messing with his girl. Shelton was ready for a fight. After the game Billy didn't shower but just changed his clothes and went out to Howard Road, where Shelton was waiting. "By the time I showered," Ted said, "and was on my way out there, cars were coming back. 'Hey, what happened?' I said. 'Where's the fight?' 'Ain't no fight,' they said. Shelton threw a couple of punches, Billy blocked them and hit Shelton several times, and he went down for the count. Here was this big, bad Marine who'd been to basic coming back to whip Billy and he was out."

On the football field, "Billy was outside linebacker. He could stick you. In college, you learn technique, which he didn't. He didn't go to the next level." Ted said Billy might not have gotten the chances other kids did because of the family he was from. "In high school there was a lot of politics. Some kids played sports because of politics. Especially in baseball there was some discrimination. When a prominent man in the community went to a game, he wanted to see his son on the diamond." Ted recalled how such a kid was a starter at second base ahead of him. In a baseball game against the Roosevelt Rough Riders, Ted didn't get into the game until the sixth inning and then he hit a home run.

"In wrestling, those kids sat on the bench," Ted said, "because they weren't tough enough. It's one-on-one out there on the mat. Only the strong survive. Wrestling is the legitimate sport. I could wrestle."

Five years after being drafted, Ted was in Europe when he learned of his high school buddy Billy's death at the hands of a woman's estranged husband. "It's sad," Ted said, "but when you understand him you respect him. He always wanted that something extra. I don't have anything negative to say about him. He was a lover. He just thought he could lay every woman. That was his downfall. You can always find trouble if you're looking for it. When they sent me to Venice, I could speak Italian and girls would come up to me, but I knew. My dad told me, 'Keep that thing in your pants.'"

The Toughest Kid We Knew

Every San Joaquin Valley high school in those years had one: the toughest kid in town. Ours was Billy Carter. Before the name was sullied by a president's brother, it seemed a perfect moniker for a fighter—Billy Carter. Almost everybody in Madera knew the name, and if you didn't you would soon find out. Prior to the era of Muhammad Ali and his rhyming challenges, Billy was known to taunt an opponent with a big grin and his own rhythmic ditty:

I'm big and bad
And I won't be had.
My ass is all red,
My nose is all snotty,
If you don't know
Who you're messin' with,
You better ask somebody.
Come and get Carterized!

The big smile then vanished; fists and feet flew.

I first heard of Billy Carter when I was in elementary school while waiting with classmates on the lawn near the high school malt shop called the Coyote Den. We were country kids who attended the parochial school in town and had permission to take a high school bus home since our school had none. I think we had to sit together in the front seats to protect us from further education by high school students. While waiting for the bus we learned about the thirteen-year-old boy from another elementary school, who came to the Coyote Den and called down high school boys. "Billy never shied away from a fight," a friend recalled, "but he was no bully. He took on the toughest kids. He told me to always go for the biggest guy because then if you got whipped you had an excuse."

Billy himself wasn't huge, but he was scrappy and fast. Nine out of ten times, friends recall, he got in the first punch or kick. His good balance allowed him to throw punches while kicking, which was okay in the noble sport of valley fistfighting. Knives and guns weren't okay.

One night Billy was sitting with high school friends in Mary's Café, the all-night joint where we often went for something to eat in the early morning after dragging main or partying at the lake. What happened was a lesson in eye contact—what you could say with your eyes. A guy on a stool at the counter glared at Billy. Billy stared back with his transparent blue eyes. The next thing you knew, the guy—he didn't seem to know Billy from anyone—sauntered over to the booth and said, "Do you want to square this away out back or what?"

Billy replied politely, "Well, yeah, if you'd like to."

The guy had on a leather jacket, and out back he started to take it off when the fight began. The guy only got his jacket halfway off before the fight was over.

"That guy was stupid" was the assessment some forty years later when four of us sat in a Madera café eating breakfast. A manager of a water district, an owner of a tractor company, a county land assessor, and I were talking about Billy. Important aspects of street fighting in those years were misdirection and deception—the wily arts of the coyote—and Billy was a master of them. He wasn't a boxer; he never put on boxing gloves for the annual Madera High School Punch Bowl—boxing entailed set rules and discipline. Billy was a brawler who invented the rules as he went along. He'd hit with blows you didn't see coming, and you never knew from what part of his body they might come. He could dance on one foot while kicking with the other, spin around, crack you in the jaw with a left elbow, followed by a right fist. Such moves were pretty to see, if you weren't receiving them. He understood the elements of war in relation to street fighting better than anyone we knew. Before a big fight he worked himself up to a pitch so at the right moment there was an explosion of adrenaline and he overwhelmed his opponent, as on the night he fought Johnny Díaz. Word had come that Johnny was looking for Billy, who sat in a booth in Mary's Café, glancing this way and that, hardly able to sit still, working himself into a frenzy. When Johnny showed up and they went outside, Billy jammed him against a chain-link fence and threw so many blows Johnny couldn't retaliate.

The thing about Billy was that he hated to lose. If a bigger, older guy started getting the better of him he wouldn't quit. He kept coming on until the other guy gave up. Billy just had to win.

The fight that elevated his legend was with Joe Rosales. Billy was still young, maybe a sophomore, and Joe, out of school, was known in those days as a good baseball player and a tough pachuco—not only tough but a mean son of a bitch. Nobody wanted to mess with Joe.

The fight took place at night in the parking lot of the Safeway supermarket. Margaret Jones Sellai was a freshman, driving by the store with her father that night, when her dad turned to her and said, "Billy's in a fight," a casual remark revealing Billy's intimate place in the social awareness of a tightly knit small town.

In the parking lot, Billy saw that his arm was cut. Joe had pulled a straight razor. Billy stared at his arm in disbelief, then charged Joe and the razor. Few had seen Billy beat up somebody with such ferocity, and the guys had to pull him off.

Often fights were more ritualistic, especially between friends. Roy Jones, who was eating breakfast with us, remembered how he fought Billy three times and lost three times. "I could outbox him, but I couldn't outfight him." Roy later boxed during basic training at Fort Ord. The other three of us eating breakfast—Don, Frank, and I—had wrestled on college teams but hadn't boxed. Roy recalled how once he thought he had a chance to whip Billy. They were driving around in Billy's car, passing back and forth a jug of port sweetened with Kool-Aid powder. When it came Roy's turn, he didn't drink. He tipped the jug to his lips and blew bubbles, then watched Billy continue to drain the jug. When the wine went way down, Roy saw his chance and slugged Billy. The car jerked to a stop. They both jumped out of the car and started fighting, as they had in the past, but this time another friend in the back seat, a high school tennis player, pushed between them—"Hey, you guys are friends," he shouted—and accidentally got hit in the throat, flopped to the ground, and started twitching. Billy and Roy stopped fighting and knelt over him. That was the end of the fight.

In the mountains at Bass Lake, Billy's expanding reputation brought guys from other towns to fight him during the weekend dances. Once, he was scheduled to square off against an Indian from North Fork, a Mono named Floyd Lavell. The fight was arranged two weeks in advance to take place by the falls. Billy wore shin-high combat boots and a sweatshirt, which he took off and handed to Roy, who was acting as a sort of second. Floyd— and Roy remembers that he was a *big* Indian—swung at Billy, who pulled back, slipping the punch that smashed between Roy's eyes. Blood spurted all over his face. Billy and Floyd stopped fighting, shook hands, and turned their attention to Roy.

The only fights that came close to being lethal were between Billy and his older brother. No rules or restrictions restrained those battles. Archie had beat up Billy when he was young, and Billy later returned the favor, once by grabbing a lawn sprinkler—the kind that whirls around—and whipping his brother, Roy said, "to within an inch of his life." Another time Billy stabbed Archie deep in the back with a sharp-pointed school compass. Don recalled a classic battle between the brothers out at his dad's ranch. Billy got on top of his brother and was trying to poke out his eyes when Archie clamped his teeth on Billy's finger. They both got to their feet with Billy's mangled finger still lodged in Archie's mouth. Friends pulled them apart, and Billy ran into the house. By the time he returned from the kitchen with a butcher knife, the other boys had gotten Archie into a car and off the ranch.

Billy got nicknamed (or nicknamed himself) Billy Butcher, as he pummeled more and more guys at Bass Lake. He knocked Roger Preston over the balcony and into the lake. "Roger had no business tangling with Billy," Frank said as we ate breakfast. Billy wouldn't boast about such a feat.

"He wasn't a show-off or a braggadocio," Don said.

"I don't remember Billy ever making an achievement out of fighting," Frank added.

Billy's stories about his exploits were often indirect and amusing. During one 3:00 a.m. Sunday morning breakfast of sausage and eggs at the counter of Mary's Café, Billy showed me the deep cut below his knuckle. While fighting that night at the lake he'd thrown an uppercut. "The damn guy had his mouth open," Billy said. A front tooth dug through his finger to the bone. An old broken bone in his hand still gave him trouble. He often got his hands hurt more than himself, although he wasn't loath to talk about when he got whipped. He made a funny story about the time some Chowchilla cowboys had ganged up on him and he crawled under a car to escape, but they dragged him out and worked him over.

"When it didn't get into this fighting and escalation of violence," Frank remembered, "Billy was a fun guy to be around."

The men at breakfast some forty years later agreed. "He was lively," Don said. "It was nice for me because I'm quiet and subdued, you know, and he was always meeting the girls, going here and there, and making things happen. To have a guy like that around, for me, made life a lot more enjoyable and exciting. Almost all the time it was pleasurable."

"He was smart, witty, charming," Frank said.

"He had a dynamic personality," Roy added. "He held his own, he kept his word, and he always got the girl."

I mentioned that someone overhearing us might say we were romanticizing a violent punk.

"If you want to think Billy Carter was a punk," Frank said, "you can probably find plenty of evidence to support your view. But Billy was no punk."

"In fact," Don said, "if you take the fights out of the equation—if you remove the stigma of fighting from his life—Billy was the All-American Boy."

I asked what he meant.

"He had crystal-clear blue eyes, a great smile, he was a hard worker, and a loyal friend."

Like the All-American Boy he also drank more milk than you could imagine. He even mixed Starlac powder into a glass of regular milk to make it thicker.

"He could make people laugh," Frank said. "He made adults laugh."

"Everybody liked Billy," Gary Bolding once told me after his own friendship with Billy had soured, "grownups, colored people, girls—everyone."

Billy moved easily through a wide swath of valley society. Besides Ted Payne, one of his buddies was Wilbert Holley, a black hurdler on the track team. Others were players on the football team, when Billy wore number 31 and did okay as an offensive and defensive end. The range of his popularity can't be dismissed. Teachers, like my aunt who taught high school English, found Billy clean-cut and well mannered. He wasn't a great student, my aunt told me, but he was polite and mature, even when he clowned around, which he often did in a good-spirited way. Ted Payne's father called him "amenable," a kid "well liked" in the black community because he was never arrogant but you couldn't run over him either. He was the sort of boy adults wanted to help. When a high school social science teacher and tennis coach tried to get Billy to think about not getting into so much trouble, Billy replied, "Sometimes I just gotta fight, Coach. I don't know why, I just gotta fight."

A friend of Billy's once told me, "You can't leave out the pleasure of fighting." The friend is a gentle man, a keeper of bees, in fact. "There's no better feeling," he added, "than kicking the shit out of somebody."

His wife looked at him incredulously, as if to say, "None? None in the world?"

Billy fought the way a binge drinker drinks—in raging bursts. The well of anger that nourished his outbursts was narrow and deep and didn't spill over into other parts of his life, but to maintain his equilibrium he apparently had to vent his fury by taking the opportunity every now and then to bash someone.

Like the binge drinker who's sweet when sober, Billy when not fighting was funny and easy with friends and charming to adults and girls.

"He was a magnet for girls," Frank said, "no doubt about that."

All of us at breakfast recalled that dealing with high school girls in those years wasn't easy; in fact, as Frank said, it was damn hard, but Billy had a knack. He was no more afraid of girls than of other guys. While we gawked with our hands in our pockets, he was talking and making them laugh. Being Billy's friend as a guy meant that the girls swarmed around. He was good-looking, sure, but part of the attraction, of course, had to do with his power, as it did for us, his valor and excellence as a warrior, understood in the primal sense of $\alpha\rho\varepsilon\tau\eta$, or virtue, in the Homeric epics. There had to be some danger there—that's sexy—but not too much—that's scary. In fact, when recently looking at the senior photo of Billy in the high school yearbook, I was startled to notice for the first time how closely he resembled the young, confident, handsome outlaw Johnny Dillinger. For the girls Billy's dangerousness was mostly offstage. I recently could find only one woman who had actually seen him fight.

She told me, "My boyfriend arranged a fight out behind his garage between Billy and Bob Hatch who was Mormon and lived in my neighborhood and was nonviolent and is actually dead now from leukemia. His folks had a farm in Chowchilla and so Bob had great strength and muscles from that heavy work." The Mormon versus the Okie, two ethnic identities of the West. "Many of the senior class attended. I was connected and therefore got a front row view which after the first punch and initial sparring I abandoned and thought how stupid. Bob was suspended from school for a week and was quite bruised. I don't know about Billy. I blamed him and his peer group."

Most of the girls knew Billy at the Bass Lake dances and town parties rather than at fights. Roy recalled how he and Billy learned to dance together in the seventh grade. They bopped to Bill Haley and the Comets. They slow-danced together, with Billy being the girl and Roy the guy, then the other way around, practicing the box step—one, two, three, four—teaching each other to dance. "We did that for hours," Roy said, "till we got to where we knew all the dances." From those years, Roy still keeps a small, square snapshot of himself and Billy, crammed into a coin-operated photo booth, facing the camera, their heads side by side. By the time he was in high school, Billy adopted a style of dance called the Hydro, a sort of bop and stomp. He could lean way back, his shoulders dipping to the floor, limbo-style, while the girl danced in and out between his legs. Then the girl leaned way back. We all danced the Hydro.

One of Billy's girlfriends at the lake was the daughter of a rich businessman from the Bay Area, though he usually seemed more attracted to girls in town connected to the medical profession. He dated a doctor's daughter and a dentist's daughter in what we then thought were the ritzy suburbs. Billy lived on the other side of town in a sparsely furnished brick house where he ate a lot of beans, corn bread, Okie food. "Billy was pure Okie," Frank said. "He wasn't that far from the Dust Bowl. He was as Okie as you can get."

His real name was Orville Lee Carter, though nobody called him that. He had been born in Texas and migrated to the valley with his family when he was five.

"To a doctor, Billy was Spam-eating trailer trash," Roy's brother told me. "A doctor wouldn't want him around his daughter. Hell, would you? Would you want Billy Carter running around with your daughter? I wouldn't. I'd have killed the son of a bitch, if he'd come around my daughter."

I talked to the dentist's daughter, who said that even though her dating was restricted as a freshman she got to go out with Billy because her mother liked him so much. I went to see her mother, then in her eighties, still living in the nice suburban house Billy had visited when he dated her daughter.

"All the girls liked Billy," the woman said. "I think they liked his snazzy car."

I remember Billy's pink Oldsmobile parked across the street when I picked up my date in a car borrowed from my parents.

Another was a remodeled blue '36 Ford coupe with a rumble seat and a stick shift on the floor. Billy drove distinctive cars. Later he also rode a motorcycle.

I asked the dentist's wife about her daughter dating somebody from the other side of town with Billy's reputation. "Billy was a very thoughtful boy," she replied.

Jerry Weinberger, the son of a doctor at the time, now a professor, reflected on the porous social borders we lived in. "I still remember," he told me, "how my first visit to a classmate's home in the first or second grade was to a labor camp tent. How in Scarsdale would that happen? My take is that Madera was a snapshot of the USA--Okie Dust Bowl migration, Italian immigration, Armenian immigration, Mexican underclass and middle class, black underclass, et cetera—the town was so small that one part couldn't but share the life experiences of the other parts. There was no rich suburban isolation. The kids from the top, such as it was, went to school, cheek by jowl, with the kids from the bottom. Nobody I know from academia, where you and I spent our lives, has ever known the likes of Gary Bolding or Billy Carter. I'm glad I did."

Clay Daulton recalls a high school dance party at the home of one of the valley's biggest and richest ranchers. Billy was dancing with the doctor's daughter when he lifted her up over his head and she straightened out stiff as a board. He held her up high with both hands, Clay said, and then very slowly brought her down to his head and chest, put her on the floor, and resumed dancing.

From the girls in Madera we learned what a sweet-talker Billy was, which impressed us immensely in those years, since we were so often tongue-tied and fearful of being trapped by wily women. If you confessed affection for a girl, the next thing you knew she had your high school ring, wrapped with thread and enameled with clear nail polish to fit her own finger, and you were stuck. You were going steady. No wonder it was hard and frightening to say "I love you" and sound sincere. I remember the dentist's daughter being in a swoon because Billy had told her with all the right enunciations and pauses something like "The way I feel… makes me think…I must be…in love," and I recall musing at the time, "That's so cool. Why couldn't I have thought of that?"

The doctor's daughter recently told me, "I don't think I ever talked to a woman who didn't like Billy. He even charmed my stepmother, and that took a lot. He knew what to say, when to say it, and how to say it. I don't know where he learned that anymore than where he learned to fight."

Billy, like his brother, had the gift of gab. I was just beginning to write stories at the time, and I was taken with his tall tales and inventive phrasing. I can see him now, leaning back against the fender of a car under the bright summer lights at the Big-Top Drive-In, laughing and telling stories. Guys in groups were known to get gross, and Billy's stories could match their raunchiness, though not without wit. He said he was forming a new 4Cs in the valley. 4Cs was shorthand for the Central California Commercial College, a two-year business college my father had attended. Billy's 4Cs referred to the Central California Crotch Cannibals, of which he proclaimed himself founder and president. He apparently had a lot of responsibility as president to uphold high standards. "I was practicing the other night," he told us, "but went on too long, and my sticky eyes gummed shut by the time I got home, and I had to wake my mom to steam them open with a teakettle."

Once, Frank's brother, Ray, told me that he thought Billy should have been an actor; in fact, he said, Billy *was* an actor, and the valley was his stage.

"He was a take-charge guy," one of the men at breakfast said. We talked about the time on the way home from the lake when a Corvette with three girls flipped, threw one from the car, and landed on top of the other two, pinning them under the convertible. Billy arrived and told a bunch of guys to help him lift the car, but adults wouldn't let them do it, saying it was too dangerous, the car might fall back on the girls. Billy persisted, and as the town newspaper reported, the two girls "were freed by passersby" and survived. Janice, the girl who'd been thown from the car, was dead. She and her brother had lived a mile from me when I was a child, the nearest playmates I had at that time. I was with her brother that night when we got the call that his sister had been killed in a wreck on the way home from the lake. She was seventeen. We were all at her funeral, for most of us the saddest we'd ever attended.

The men at the table said that Billy was always there to help you. If you had a date and needed cash, he would shell out five bucks so you could get a Coke or cherry lime rickey at the Big Top. Of course, he expected you to return the favor. Frank recalled when he was in the fourth grade and some toughs were threatening to jump him, Billy got word and walked home with him. "He didn't have to do that," Frank said. "He was good-hearted."

Ray April told me that one night out in the country in an irrigated vineyard, some seniors, including Billy, were hazing him and some fellow freshmen, as was the annual custom at Madera High. The seniors made the freshmen line up and strip to their underpants in preparation for a run through mud. Behind him, Ray heard one of the crazier kids say, "Let's shove these firecrackers up their asses." With a sidelong glance over his shoulder, Ray saw Billy cock his fist at the guy with the firecrackers. Billy's gesture ended the threat. "Billy was like that," Ray said. "He kept guys from getting out of line."

"The one thing he wouldn't do," Roy said, "and I think I'm remembering this right, is that he wouldn't try to embarrass you. He would fight you, but when he was telling his stories he wouldn't use you as the butt of a joke to impress a bunch of guys."

You could tease him, too. Don remembered how some football players put wintergreen in Billy's jockstrap, and he had to excuse himself from the practice field to go take a shower. Guys weren't afraid to do that sort of thing to him because he would take it in good humor.

Not everyone remembers him this way. Roy's older brother, who came to the table where we were eating, was leery. "You couldn't trust him a hundred percent," George Jones said. "He'd go off on you in a heartbeat. I always kept him in front of me." We recalled when Billy lost his temper and jumped our friend Jim Unti in the town park at dusk one evening after he mistakenly thought Jim had splattered him with a water balloon. Jim stood his ground, throwing blows. Later while drinking with Billy, Frank reprimanded him for wrongly beating on Jim and slugged him in the stomach. Billy didn't retaliate.

George, who was a strong swimmer and boxer in high school, fought Billy a couple of times and beat him a couple of times, he says. Once in the Madera High gym, the coaches said that whoever stayed inside the big circled M on the floor would win. George, who was older, bigger, and in better shape than Billy at the time, used his boxing skills to pop Billy and then dance to safety outside the circle. "Billy would not come out of that circle," George said. "He would do anything to win. He thought he was winning by staying in the circle and getting hit. But afterward he told everyone I whipped him."

Another time when Roy and Billy were freshmen, three guys jumped them near the swimming pool park, and one flashed a knife. Billy grabbed a limb and pulled himself up into a tree, while Roy ran to Yosemite Avenue to get his older brother, who was dragging main. George came to the park, where the guys still had Billy treed. Billy jumped down, and he and George whipped the three of them.

What made Billy fight?

"His brother," George says. "His father and mother—they were both alcoholics. Billy had to fight to survive. He had to fight his dad, he had to fight his mom, he had to fight his brother."

That's part of it. What took me years to understand was the social magnitude of Billy's fighting, the deep well of anger embedded in the sons and daughters of Steinbeck's Okies, the rage rising from the internalized social stigma shared with their Dust Bowl parents of being told: you're not good enough, you're still second pickings. A temptation to reduce their fighting to personal, pent-up, testosterone-charged rage misses the migrant Okie experience. Denigrated by those with money and status, poor Okie kids had their pride and fists, as well as an ingrained thousand-year Scots-Irish tradition of toughness and fighting that had helped fire the genes of hardscrabble frontiersmen and gunslingers from Daniel Boone to Davy Crockett to Kit Carson to Wyatt Earp to Belle Starr. You could look down your noses at them, but their fists could break those noses.

"Billy had to fight for everything he got," George said, "but he wanted something more. He had a lot of potential. By the time he was nineteen, he had his own business, and a damn successful one, too."

That business was the Carter Septic Tank Company he was running for his dad. Billy was a honey-pumper, as we said back then. "There's no better business than pumping honey," he once told me, "except maybe the restaurant business. People always got to do one or the other."

George Jones said, "Billy would get up in the morning and go to work. He was a self-starter, and he worked hard. Nobody had to wake his ass up. He did everything with gusto. He didn't hold back. Everything he got he worked for."

Roy said that when they were kids Billy got him a job at a gas station where they worked together on the midnight-to-eight shift. He also got Roy a job out on the ranch of Don's dad, where they were both irrigators from sunup to sundown. Billy started spending a lot of time on the ranch, partying on the weekends. Don's dad had a jeep they drove around, shooting rabbits.

Billy admired Don's dad, his ranch, his nice home, his swimming pool, and once told Roy in a wistful voice, "Man, someday…" He wanted things like that; he wanted money, he wanted to be noticed, though Roy says "he sometimes feared he wouldn't be good enough." Not lost on Billy, no doubt, was that Don's dad had it both ways: he was successful and wild; he worked hard and played hard: he ranched, drank, fought, gambled, and chased the girls. With him and a lot of valley ranchers, I think of a view they shared with a character in a short story by the Russian writer Isaac Babel, who said how the wisdom of his ancestors was firmly lodged in his head: we are born to enjoy our work, our fights, our loves; we are born for that and for nothing else.

One night, Don's dad was driving home from a bar when his car went out of control, rolled down an embankment, and burst into flames. Don's dad was thrown from the car and pinned under the front tire until a passerby lifted the burning car off him. Two days later Don's dad died of burns. He was fifty-six.

"Billy never realized his own potential," George said. "Look at his brother, Archie; he eventually became a millionaire twice over building shopping malls, and Billy always outdid his brother. Those guys were smart. They had Okie intelligence. Billy could look at you and read you in a minute. He could tell what you wanted and see that you got it. When he was older, he could've never worked for somebody. He only played the game if he could run the show. He could make other guys do whatever he wanted. He would have Roy here sitting down in a septic, spraying the walls with a hose, shit splattering all over him, for twenty bucks a week."

"Twenty bucks and all the Pepsi I could drink," Roy added. "That seemed pretty good in those days."

"I mean, the guy was smart," George repeated.

I mentioned how another friend of ours once told me, "Billy was a magnification of us all."

Roy nodded. "That hits it," he said, then added in unison with Don, "or what all of us *wanted* to be."

A friend of mine, who didn't grow up in the valley and didn't know Billy, advised me to explore the counterview of Billy as a dangerous sociopath. "A lot of sociopaths can be quite charming," he said.

Another friend read these pages while I was writing. She told me, "I don't like this Billy Carter story. All the women are locked into romantic fantasies and the guys into homoerotic feelings."

Well, maybe that's part of it, though a one-sided part. Not all toughs, and fewer sociopaths, elicit such affection forty years later, and not just from four guys reminiscing at breakfast. After a reading of this story for the Madera library, over half the audience, both men and women, raised their hands when asked if they knew Billy, including the dentist's daughter and Jim Unti, who recounted in his usual wry way the water-balloon confrontation with Carter. People in that group didn't apply labels; they told stories.

While writing this piece, I had a dream about Billy, the only one I ever recall having. We were in a Catholic church, the one we attended for our friend's funeral after her car crash. The only other time I think we were in a church together—a Protestant church—was back in high school when a friend of ours married a girl from another town he'd gotten pregnant at our New Year's Eve party. In my dream I walked up the aisle and saw Billy leaning against the wall with his arms folded across his chest, looking relaxed and comfortable with himself in the way of a resting cat. I awaited the nod that guys in the high school hallways liked to get from him to show that he knew them—a lifting of the chins, maybe, exchanged between guys like a signal between members of a secret society. In my dream, Billy noticed me and smiled in a way that made me realize that *he* generated the affection we were still returning forty years later. I was glad to see him, but he also was glad to see me. In my dream, we were glad to see each other.

After high school, most of us didn't see Billy so often as we scattered to various places. He was running his dad's business, and serving in the National Guard. Roy recalls that he was even an auxiliary deputy sheriff. "They figured if you couldn't beat him, you might as well get him to join you." Billy still had fights. "Guys wanted to fight him for no reason at all," Roy said, "just because he was Billy Carter. He told me he got to a point where he couldn't back out. I don't know, he felt he had to fight back, or he would've tarnished something."

One night, when I was back in the valley from college, Billy and I got together. We were drinking beer, and he said, "Let's go to Fresno. I'm going to get in the last fucking fight of my life." We went to a pool hall, where Billy bumped into a couple of guys around the table, but nothing happened. They seemed to know him, and Billy's heart wasn't in it. He had to get up early to go to work. "Let's go home," he said.

"He was getting more serious," the doctor's daughter told me, "more sophisticated." Billy was married with a little boy and another child on the way. He and the doctor's daughter had planned to get married, but her parents intervened. Without her knowledge, they called Billy over to their house and told him he wasn't good enough.

The woman he did marry was the daughter of a Portuguese American rancher and had been a high school majorette. "He wanted to build up a business," the doctor's daughter said, "similar to his dad's and take it into Fresno and the mountains. I don't think he would look for fights anymore, although he wouldn't back away."

The doctor's daughter had separated from her own husband and had begun seeing Billy again. Though she had started divorce proceedings, she stayed in touch with her husband, who wanted a reconciliation. They had a four-year-old daughter. One evening, Billy and his friend Charlie, who worked for him, stopped by her apartment and they all went to a bar for a few beers. She told Billy she'd been with her husband that day and that when Billy had phoned earlier, Gary, who was known as an unflappable, easygoing guy, got upset and threatened to shoot him, but Billy just laughed it off. Back in the apartment, she and Billy were in the kitchen getting something to eat when the doorbell rang. Charlie opened the door, and a man pushed the barrel of a snub-nosed .38-caliber pistol into his stomach.

"Who is it?" Billy yelled from the kitchen.

"I don't know," Charlie yelled back.

When Billy appeared in the kitchen doorway, Gary swung the pistol and shot at him but missed. Billy charged Gary, who fired two more shots. Billy groaned and dropped to the floor. Gary turned and shot at Charlie, who managed to escape into the bathroom and climb out the window. As he ran to call the police, Charlie heard more shots.

While Gary was reloading the pistol, Billy got to his feet and grabbed an end table, knocking a lamp and magazines to the floor. Using the table as a shield, he backed into a bedroom and locked the door. Gary was still reloading the pistol when his wife came into the living room and tried to stop him. "I can kill you, too," he shouted. He pushed her against the wall, then raised his foot and kicked open the bedroom door. Billy appeared in the doorway, and Gary backed up, firing the pistol. Billy dropped to the floor. Gary bent over and shot him in the head behind the ear. He then pointed the pistol toward his wife and fired two shots that slammed into the wall behind her. On the way back to Madera, he rolled his pickup. He got a ride with a truck driver to the hospital, where he was arrested.

Gary Bolding was convicted of voluntary manslaughter and served just over three years in prison. The defense had portrayed

Billy as a proficient street fighter, who reportedly carried a knife and had a penchant for violence, someone Gary had reason to fear. After his release from prison, Frank and I went to visit Gary in his apartment. It was a warm summer night, and we sat in a dark, screened-in porch. Gary retold the story mechanically. He said the trial was like a play that didn't have much to do with what had happened. To him everything seemed like a bad dream, and he could only remember parts of it. He couldn't believe what had gotten into him. Like everyone else, he said, he'd once liked Billy and had even run around with him. He regretted what had happened. "I wish Billy was alive," he said.

Frank felt that Gary, despite his words, seemed cold about killing Billy. Frank had learned of Billy's death in a letter from his mother when he was in the army in Germany. The news had come close after the assassinations of Martin Luther King and Robert Kennedy, and the world seemed to be cracking apart. Frank felt shaken. *What the hell?* he thought.

I, too, was shaken. I remember one late autumn night in Harvard Square, talking with a friend from Madera who had also ended up in graduate school there. My friend shrugged and said, "Live by the sword, die by the sword." Maybe he was only covering up other feelings, but I recall how his response left me feeling deadened.

Billy's brother, Archie, went on the skids after Billy's death. People said he quit caring about anything. His drinking got real bad, his business crashed, and he went bankrupt.

Billy's wife, Dina, remained bitter about Gary Bolding not getting his just due. She never remarried. When I asked her brother Marty about her ongoing affection for Billy, he said, "Sometimes the flame never dies." I pointed out that Billy had been running around with another woman at the time. Marty shrugged it off. "Ah, that was just a fling." Forty days after the shooting, Billy's son was born. Dina named him Billy Jr. Marty offered this explanation about his sister's feelings for her murdered husband: "Billy was full of love, you know." Dina died in Nevada before I could talk to her about this story. Her grandson is also named Billy Carter.

Roy Jones recalls how a few years after Billy's death he and his wife went to Farnesi's Restaurant and bumped into Gary Bolding at the bar. Gary asked Roy to come outside. Roy didn't know what was up. He walked into the dark parking lot, and Gary turned toward him, holding his arms straight by his sides, and said, "Okay, do what you have to do."

"What the hell are you talking about?" Roy asked.

"I killed your friend. Go ahead, do what you have to do."

Roy replied, "Gary, you did your time. I'm not going to do anything."

Gary started to sob, arms by his sides, tears streaking his face. Some years later, he died of cancer. He was forty-eight.

Roy told us that every Sunday at Mass during prayers for the dead, he remembers two people, Billy Carter and Hurdy Jung. "Billy for his violent death, and Hurdy for his violent death." Both were his high school friends, and both had been shot. "I'm wondering," Roy said, "if in that time before the Lord took him, did Billy have a chance to repent and say, 'Lord, I want to accept you as my savior'? Did he have a chance? The same with Hurdy, even though he was Buddhist. In that hour of need, in that last moment, was there still hope and a chance?"

The police report says that Billy was shot four times—in the leg, the shoulder, the throat, and the head. The way he was found lying in the hall with his feet at the bedroom doorway indicates that he came out of the bedroom toward the gun. The police report says that his right arm was cocked toward his head, his hand doubled into a fist. He was twenty-seven.

Basque Family Style

Eating family style in California's San Joaquin Valley when I was growing up meant sitting at a long, noisy table with people you might not know and eating food you hadn't ordered.

Family style! Or, in the style of the family. What families best define this way of eating? In the San Joaquin Valley, the answer came quick: "Why, that's Basque family style." The irony of those three Delphic words, *Basque…Family…Style*, apparently understandable to everyone in the valley, is that the long communal tables at Basque hotels began as a rooming house custom for boarders. In other words, family style was invented for men without families, mostly unmarried Basque sheepherders.

Sunday afternoons for me as a boy often meant going to the Basque Hotel or the Santa Fe Hotel in Fresno. Since my family lived on a ranch twenty-five miles away, such a drive in those days was a trek. The Santa Fe Hotel sat across from the Santa Fe Railroad Depot, while the redbrick Basque Hotel was built near the Southern Pacific tracks, where incoming trains dropped off herders. Both hotels offered to a child visions of spectacular bars in darkened rooms where families met relatives and friends for drinks before dinner. The wall behind the bar of the Basque Hotel held multicolored liquor bottles and two large recessed panels with illuminated blown-up photos of sheep bands. I remember one ghostly black-and-white photo of a huge flock drinking from a mountain stream.

My grandfather, mother, father, and aunt drank picons. The bartender's quick hands packed ice into glasses, poured liquid from three different bottles—brandy, grenadine, and Amer Picon, an aperitif laced with the taste of orange, gentian, and quinine. The concoction was topped with club soda sprayed from a bar hose, then stirred with a long spoon. The rims of the glasses were rubbed with twists of lemon peel. I was always offered a sip. First came the heady fumes, then the fruity, bittersweet taste. Now called "picon punch," a term I never heard as a child, these drinks to me remain simply *picons*. Popular in the Basque Country at the turn of the twentieth century but now virtually unavailable there, picons evolved into the Basque ethnic drink of the American West.

While the adults hobnobbed, I sneaked around the bar, down a dark hall past the toilets, through a door, a meat-cutting room—I could already hear shouts and the slaps of the hand-ball—another door, and into the huge concrete court—a fronton or *kantxa*—roofed with wire grating, where men with bare palms whacked a handball against the walls in a vicious game of pelota. Or at least it seemed vicious to me as the hard rubber ball violently caromed around the court.

I was somehow connected to these strange men playing pelota. My mother was Basque. Her parents were born in the Basque Country, and yet in those years I scarcely knew how we all were connected. Neither did these men, at least in terms of a common ethnic history. Euskara was a guttural language to my young ear, dotted with *tx* and *k* and *z* in words such as *artzainak* (sheepherders) and *txakurrak* (sheepdogs). Basques called their European home Euskal Herria—the land of Euskara speakers— the region that straddles the spine of the western Pyrenees between France and Spain down to the Bay of Biscay, the same area where the Romans first encountered them. The Basque hotels of the West became educational centers where these *Euskaldunak* from Spain and France often learned about each other in ways they wouldn't have in Europe. They had become *Amerikanuak*—Basques in America.

Like Greek coffeehouses in Utah, Basque hotels in California and Nevada were both cultural havens and transitional zones of assimilation for immigrants. Normally located, as I mentioned, along the railroad tracks of a Western town within sight of the depot, the Basque hotel served as a rooming house, post office, card room, dance hall, convalescent ward, unemployment hospice, and retirement community for these ersatz families in the agricultural West. They also became business centers and hiring halls for traveling Basque sheep owners. The concept of "family" expanded as Basques began to invite friends for dinner, such as Béarnais sheepmen, whose homeland adjoined the Basque Country, and other immigrant agricultural workers in the ethnically rich San Joaquin Valley. Eventually the hotels opened up their boarders' tables to the public.

The first Basque hotel in the West was built in California during the gold rush in the 1850s. Others popped up in Nevada, Idaho, and Oregon, then in the rest of the intermountain West. At one time there were eight in Stockton. In the 1970s, six remained in a three-block area of San Francisco's North Beach. Bakersfield still has three restaurants. Typically two stories, a Basque hotel has lodgings upstairs and a barroom and a dining room downstairs. Today's more common family-style Basque restaurants seat parties at individual tables. Many hotel-restaurants are in transition. Now at the boarders' table, people often have a choice of entrées. To a purist, once choice and a menu come to hand, the eating is no longer family style.

—⁓—

At the Fresno Basque Hotel, when the dinner bell rang, we streamed into the dining room. Latecomers were out of luck.

Down the long table, stacked with open bottles of red wine, came steaming bowls and platters in four or five courses, soup first. I loved to slather a crusty hunk of sourdough bread with butter and soak it in the vegetable soup. My other favorite was the shrimp potato salad. When years later I ate a Sunday afternoon meal at a long table with my relatives at the Hotel Vega in the Basque Country of Spain, there was no shrimp potato salad—my relatives hadn't heard of such a thing—but there were plenty of other fish dishes, such as *merluza* cheeks, from the Bay of Biscay, where, as I was told, the seafood is tastier and fresher because, of course, the water is neither too cold nor too hot. I don't remember fish at the Basque Hotel, except *bacalao*, the slabs of dry, salted cod, stiff as boards, that Basques claim is tastier after soaking than the bland fresh fish. The food in hotels was touched in style by what was cooked in the sheep camps of the West: things from the pot—beans, such as garbanzos and favas, and stews without separately created complementary sauces. Sheep camp cooks allowed ingredients in cast-iron pots and skillets to condense into natural, full-bodied sauces. Such food came to be identified as American Basque, characterized in the hotels as hearty and cheap.

On the wall of the Basque Hotel hung an enlarged photograph of men eating at the hotel during a meeting of the California Woolgrowers Association. My grandfather was in the photo, not my Basque grandfather, but my father's father, born in California, who then sat at the table with me. When I looked into William Douglass and Jon Bilbao's historical study, *Amerikanuak: Basques in the New World* (1975), I discovered that my grandparents, born in the Basque Country, who owned a hotel and store in Battle Mountain, Nevada, fit the book's description of hotel proprietors who went directly from the sheep business (and, in my grandfather's case, also mining) into ownership of a commercial hotel without passing through the boardinghouse phase. But my Basque grandparents are not mentioned in the book. Ironically, this book about American Basques mentions my Béarnais American grandfather, Prosper Bergon, as someone whose biography underscores the similarity in the life experiences of Basque and Béarnais sheepmen. Where one encounters Basques in the West, the book says, one is likely to encounter Béarnais. I might have also been sitting near my Béarnais great-grandmother's brother and his wife, born in France, then ranchers south of Fresno, whose son, Henry, though ten years younger than my father, was actually my grandfather's first cousin, which, as I've said, was all very confusing to me. Next to them might have sat two old people I called Mom and Pop Lee, actually no relation at all—typical mysteries of this thing called family style.

"Save room for the chicken," someone always said as we chowed down on the other dishes. According to *Amerikanuak*, in rural Basque society, banquets on special occasions would most certainly include garbanzos, a stew dish, and chicken. American Basque hotels came to serve Old World Basque festive cuisine as ordinary fare, with an additional meat dish as an everyday staple of these multicourse meals. By the time platters of fried chicken made their way down the table, it was hard to eat more than three or four pieces. The chicken was delicious, but the prior meat dishes, usually more than one, rich in sauce, were better— lamb stew or sweetbreads or sliced tongue or pigs' knuckles or beef brains or lambs' feet or tripe in tomato and garlic sauce.

What families really eat this way? When I lived in a ranch house with my mother, father, aunt, grandfather, and sister, we sometimes ate as a main course a platter of plump chickens' feet or beef stew with a lot of round bones from which my grandfather taught me to dig out the sweet marrow. As in Basque hotels, we weren't big on desserts, except ice cream and custards. Usually

I would imitate my grandfather, who made his own dessert with the tines of a fork by mashing blue cheese and butter into a paste spread on sourdough bread, a habit he continued until his heart gave out when he was seventy-three.

On special occasions, the dinner had two meat courses. When we joined up with a neighboring Italian family, the first course might be braised doves, dozens of them, shot during the fall season. At their house, pasta came next, then maybe a roast. Quail season followed dove season, then came pheasants and ducks. The shotgun pellets that had killed the birds clattered onto people's plates as they ate. During deer season, my grandfather hung the carcass from a sycamore to skin it. In summer, when no game was in season, a first course might be sautéed frog's legs, gathered from ranch ditches and canals into burlap sacks at night with flashlights and gigs.

I have a photo of myself as a boy turning a pig on a wooden spit over a hole in the ground, my face grimacing from the heat of the coals. The occasion was the visit of Croatian friends from Nevada, where the man had worked in the mines. He and his wife—like family, as the saying goes—were my sister's godparents. I have other photos, much later ones, when I was in college, of friends and relatives at long tables under eucalyptus trees, eating a whole lamb cooked in the same way. The tables look similar to the ones my grandfather had finished building the morning of my parents' wedding, when guests returned to the ranch for an outdoor meal. I don't know what they ate, but it was probably barbecued over grape stumps, which make perfect coals. Another outdoor meal at long tables occurred when I was about to depart for graduate school. A rancher, again like family, shot a steer for the barbecue. We sawed open the skull for the brains, served as an appetizer, along with some fresh-cut mountain oysters, testicles cooked in two styles. The mountain oysters came from young rams, to be distinguished from orchids, cut from young bulls to transform them into edible steers.

Given our eating habits, it may be a little hard to understand my grandfather's response when I once served him on crackers some canned meat I'd discovered while I was still in grammar school.

"What is it?" he asked.

"Try it," I said.

He took a bite. I told him what it was. He put the cracker back on the plate and said, "Of all the goddamn meats in the world, you have to serve me rattlesnake."

Of course, it tasted like chicken. Yet this lifelong rancher and hunter couldn't tolerate what he perceived as the enemy of stock and game. Animals we kill and eat require some affection.

The golden years of the Basque Hotel, according to my family, began in the 1930s and stretched into my boyhood when Félix and Lyda Esain ran the place as an active boardinghouse with twenty-eight rooms on the second floor. In a surprising historical twist, the Fresno Basque Hotel enjoyed a later golden age, even better than the first, when a former immigrant Basque sheepherder named Fermín Achocarro Urroz bought the hotel with his wife, Margaret, and a partner in 1980.

For thirty years Fermín cooked what many of us considered the best Basque food in the San Joaquin Valley. Fermín, as his name would suggest, was born in Navarra, north of Pamplona's *Fiesta de San Fermín*, in Beinza-Labayen. After serving in Africa in the Spanish army he went to France, where in his usual cryptic way he claimed to have learned the love of cooking. He would never reveal a recipe or where in the mountains he found the best mushrooms or his secret fishing holes or how many doves he shot or how many trout he caught. "The Basque limit," he would say.

He came to the San Joaquin Valley to herd sheep when he was twenty-four, married the twenty-year-old Portuguese American Margaret Pimental when he was thirty-three, and took over running the Basque Hotel with her four years later. "Hey, New York," Fermín would call out to me from behind the bar when I entered the hotel. Without asking, he would pour me a soda and bitters. I'd written an article about the hotel for *Gastronomica: The Journal of Food and Culture*, and he thought I was also responsible for a squib in *The New York Times*, which I wasn't, but he didn't believe me. He thought I was being as misleading in my denial as he would've been.

On a March evening in 2001, when my wife, Holly, and I visited in order to write my article, fourteen years had passed since I was in the valley for my aunt's and my father's funerals, three months apart. Earlier, my Béarnais grandfather's cousin, Henry—the one younger than my father—had hosted a meal for us at the Santa Fe Hotel on the day of his mother's burial. The Santa Fe Hotel, at the time, still had boarders, about a dozen or so, mostly old men in berets, retired Basque herders. They ate by themselves at the boarders' table on weeknights, but anyone could join them for lunch or on weekends.

After the Santa Fe closed, Fermín let some of the old Basque herders into the second-floor rooms, where during his first twenty years he regularly kept boarders. No active herders now lived in the hotel, though visitors from the Basque Country sometimes stayed in the upstairs rooms. Basques now came as tourists, not herders.

During that March evening, no one played pelota anymore. Weeds grew through cracks in the concrete court. The dark barroom remained the same, still lit by those ghostly illuminated panels of sheep. Fermín still mixed picons. At 6:30 in the evening, his wife, Margaret, stepped into the bar and clanged the dinner bell, initiating a familiar nightly routine.

The bar cleared. We traipsed into the dining room to take our places at the long table, sitting in the order we entered. When I tried to leave a space for someone else, Margaret told me to move down, close up the gap. No skipping of chairs is allowed. Whoever said family style is a matter of choice? I sat next to a woman, born in Mexico, who spooned hot jalapeño salsa into her bowl of soup. I asked if the salsa was a recent innovation. I didn't remember it. Oh no, she said, it was here when her parents brought her to the hotel as a child. I was skeptical, but it made sense, since Basques, unlike other Europeans, developed a taste for the hot peppers from the Americas. Green salad, a bowl of white beans, a platter of mushrooms and peppers, and three meat dishes appeared—lamb stew, pigs' feet, and tripe—then the final dish of salty roasted beef ribs.

I saw people at individual tables eating shrimp potato salad. I asked Margaret about the salad, telling her how much I loved it as a kid, hoping to wheedle a sample from the kitchen, but was told it's served regularly only at the individual tables where people are also permitted to order entrées, although if I really wanted it, I could come back on Wednesday when it's served family style at the boarders' table. I asked why it wasn't more often served at the boarders' table. "That's the way it is," she said. I returned on Wednesday. The shrimp potato salad was as good as ever. So was the beef tongue and fried chicken served with it, family style. In the fall, Fermín always had a big dove feed, and one spring I arrived for delicious lambs' tails, provided by sheepmen. Each meal cost nine dollars.

On the March trip, I searched the room for the photo of my grandfather with the group of woolgrowers. It was gone, replaced by a large color photograph of Fermín and Margaret with ten men who were regulars at the hotel. I asked Fermín how many Basques were in the photo. He hesitated for a moment and gave me a quizzical smile. He looked amazed as he scratched his head. "Only me," he said. Four men were Japanese, others were Mexican, and, as Margaret said, Okie. "They're like family here," someone said. I sat next to a Greek American farmer and learned that his family's vineyard was not far from my old home ranch. Across from me, a rancher said his family was Basque—French Basque—who, it turned out, owned a cattle ranch near the house where my father was born when my grandfather was still a tenant farmer. Their family name, the man said, meant "the keeper of cattle." As we ate, he mentioned in passing how his father, a former regular at the hotel, had been moving five hundred head of cattle a few years earlier when his horse lay back on him and the pommel crushed his chest.

Sherbet ended the meal, but no coffee—that's a bar drink. At the bar I joined two couples from my childhood who had stopped in for after-dinner drinks. One owned a vineyard adjoining our old home ranch. The other couple was Rosemary and Mitch Lasgoity, ranchers who were my boyhood neighbors. During an earlier Friday lunch I sat next to Mitch, who was speaking Basque at the long crowded table when *bacalao* passed from hand to hand. Friday lunches were always crowded when Fermín cooked *bacalao al pil-pil*. "I hope I die before you do," Mitch told Fermín. "This tastes just like when I was a kid." Fermín laughed. At the bar, Mitch began to talk about my grandfather, my father, my mother, her Basque American brother who played basketball for the University of Nevada, her sisters. We ordered more drinks. Several years later, in 2012, Fermín died of Lou Gehrig's disease;

his servings of *bacalao al pil-pil* came to an end. Margaret put the Basque Hotel up for sale.

—⚋—

The day after that meal at the Basque Hotel, I was invited to a noon barbecue in honor of an eighty-eight-year-old Béarnais American farmer, hosted at his home ranch by his son and grandson, who invited friends from each of the three generations, about forty men in all. I knew the Sagouspe family ranch well. As a kid, I played there often with the Sagouspe children. A table held appetizers of guacamole, smoked salmon, and bowls of San Joaquin Valley almonds. Green salad, beans and garlic, various barbecued sausages, and marinated tri-tip beef roasts were served family style, with lots of wine. The farmer's grandson directed the barbecuing. We ate in the barn, and one man at each table was assigned to introduce the others seated with him.

A man stood up to begin the introductions and said, "There's a lot of history at this table—"

"No history!" our host Steve shouted from another table. "Just the names. March has only thirty-one days."

I sat next to the farmer's ninety-three-year-old brother, Jean Sagouspe, who'd driven down by himself from Oakland. "I just put it in cruise control and came down," he told me. During the first year of the Depression he herded sheep for my grandfather. "No one had any cash," he said. "Your grandfather couldn't pay me until later, but he kept me alive. Then he paid my tuition to barber and beautician school." I asked how he lived. "Your grandfather brought me flour, beans, lamb. I dug a hole and baked bread in a Dutch oven."

We got up to look at a large piece of plywood propped up in the barn and covered with family photos. In the center was an old black-and-white photo of my grandfather, Prosper, and the honored farmer's father, Pierre, holding shotguns. Strings of ducks hung between them. The limit then was twenty-five a day.

At the tables, the men talked about what farmers and ranchers always talk about, crops, weather, bad prices. Now and then the past came up, briefly, skirting nostalgia. Sam Malick, an Assyrian born in Egypt, had an old photograph of pupils at the Ripperdan country school in 1927. The farmer being feted today was in it—so were my relatives, my aunt and her stepbrother, children standing in front of the schoolhouse.

As we look at the children, men point and mention names: Yamaguchi, Logoluso, Mueller, Chun, Biscay, Sagouspe, Chávez— Japanese, Italian, German, Chinese, Basque, Béarnais, Mexican.

In the photo, next to boys with names like Roy Rodgers and Earl Rodgers are the Malicks, Gustafsons, and Arakelians— Assyrians, Swedes, and Armenians. Sigurd Lundstrom is there with Fumiko Hirahara and Socorro Verduzco.

Kazuo Goto is in the photo with my aunt, Evelyn Bergon. Years later, Kazuo would become a Methodist and a Bay Area architect who designed my aunt's house in the country and St. Joachim's Catholic Church in town.

Nothing is said about the internment camps Kazuo Goto and the other Japanese went to during the Second World War. Nothing about the history of loss, broken faith, betrayal, drunkenness, madness, suicide, and other suffering marking so many later lives of these children. We all know the stories. Today fellowship is the occasion. In certain villages of Ghana, at festive gatherings such as this one, libations are poured for those absent, the family dead. We do nothing so formal. We haven't such rituals and ceremonies. We just eat on, for the living and for the dead, silently aware of bonds stronger than those of ethnicity and geography. So we eat on, family style.

Acknowledgments

"My Basque Grandmother" was first published in the Basque Country in 2009. I'm grateful to Asun Garikano for translation of the essay into Euskara as "Nire amama euskalduna" and to Bernardo Atxaga for its publication in *Erlea*.

I'm grateful to those who read some or all of these essays in one form or another and offered helpful suggestions: Mark Bergon, Roser Caminals, Barbara Frick, Bill Heath, Ann Vernon, Kay Frauenholtz, Susanna Sturgis, William Douglass, Daryl Farmer, Zeese Papanikolas, and Jack Vernon.

My heartfelt thanks to those who gave me support or information along the way with special thanks to my lifelong valley friends Joe Claassen, Jim Unti, and Frank April, as well as Michele Karpov, Marie Grace, Judith Barrutia, Mari Carmen Arrizabalaga, Jesús Noya, David Mendive, Josephine Filippini, Aleksandra Mendive, Kon Karpov, Holland Wines, Angie Stewart, Janice Lombardi, Kaitlin Krozel, Marilyn Smith, Bernardo Arrizabalaga, Barbara Rouseyrol, Jayne Tichnor, Richard Palacioz, Virginia Yturalde, Monika Madinabeitia, David Rio, Fred Massetti, Sonny Clement, Michael Berryhill, Teri Palacioz, Tina Unti, Marc Davancens, Gene Dellavalle, Cecilia Massetti, Bill Coate, Tim Viole, Chantal Sagouspe, Bill Sterling, Cindy Martinusen, Edie Gray, Nancy Cook, Lee Mitchell, Paul Russell, Karen Lucic, Holly Hummel, Ray April, Ralph Clement, Jerry Weinberger, Coann Garvey, Sherry Daggett, Marty DeMello, Margaret Sellai, Stell Manfredi, Ronn Dominici, Richard Allen, George Jones,

Janet Allen, Roy Jones, Marie Hardin, Willie Hibdon, Don Nelson, Mike Vizcarra, Steve Sagouspe, Clay Daulton, Allen Wier, John Sellai, Diane Massetti, Joseba Zulaika, Xabier Irujo, Iñaki Arrieta, Sam Malick, Sylvan Goldberg, Aris Janigian, David Means, Don Watson, Larry Watson, Yolanda Marie Contaxis, Gretchen Skivington, Elisha Fisch, Ted Payne, Dagoberto Gilb, Jan Wrobel, Liz Dunn, Dan Whistler, Commander Bill Ward, Mona Alvarez, and Rainbow Morgan.

At the University of Nevada Press I want to thank everyone who helped shepherd this book into print, with a special nod to interim director Sandra Ott, marketing manager Sara Hendricksen, designer Iris Saltus, and production editor Sara Vélez. Special thanks also to Madeline Bergon for the author portrait and to Chris Fenner for helping to bring the cover to fruition.

Once again, to Holly St. John Bergon I owe my deepest gratitude for her advice about every detail, nearly every word, of this book.